COUNSELOR
in the
CLASSROOM

Activities and Strategies
For an Effective Classoom Guidance Program

Pat Schwallie-Giddis

David Cowan

Dianne Schilling

Cover design: Dave Cowan
Illustrations: Dianne Schilling

Copyright ©1993, (Revised, 2013) Innerchoice Publishing • All rights reserved

ISBN-10: 1-56499-085-3

ISBN-13: 978-1-56499-085-3

INNERCHOICE Publishing
15079 Oak Chase Court
Wellington, FL 33414

www.InnerchoicePublishing.com

Experience sheets may be reproduced in quantities sufficient for distribution to students in classrooms utilizing COUNSELOR in the CLASSROOM activities. All other reproduction by any means or for any purpose whatsoever, is explicitly prohibited without written permission. Requests for permission should be directed to INNERCHOICE PUBLISHING.

COUNSELOR
in the **CLASSROOM**

Contents

Welcome to Counselor in the Classroom 1

How to Use Counselor in the Classroom 17

Counselor and Teacher Activities

Who is the Counselor? 25

Validations 29

Images of Me 32

Feeling Faces 35

The Ups and Downs of Feelings 38

The Roller-Coaster Ride of Life 40

Construction Teams 42

Pictures Speak Words 44

Outline for Friendship 46

What I Want in a Friend 49

A Commercial Friendship Break 50

Do I Have a Friend for You! 52

Responding Assertively to Peer Pressure 54

How to Handle Bullies, Chicken-Callers, and
Other Peers Who Pressure You! 59

How To Handle Bully Behavior 61

Sending I Messages 64

Developing Listening Skills 69

Active Listening 72

Listening to Directions 73

Asking for Help 76

The Help Line! 79
Control Yourself! 80
Being Comfortable in School 83
Developing Classroom Rules 86
A Safety Quiz 89
What Would You Do? 91
Identities and Actions: A Lesson in Safety 93
Safety Mapping 96
Safely Home Alone 98
Safety Tips for Being Home Alone 100
Centering and Balancing 101
The Stress Basket 105
Stress Breaks 107
De-Stressing the Test 109
How to Handle Test Anxiety 111
Many Paths: An Exercise in Critical Thinking 112
Making Decisions 115
Decisions, Decisions! 118
Dear Class... Practice in Problem Solving 120
Problem-Solving Flow Chart 123
Targeting Short-Term Goals 124
Keep An Eye on Your Goal! 127
Charting the Future: Individual Goal Setting 128
Living My Goals 130
Words to Grow On 131
Strength Bombardment 134
Linked Together 136
The Take on Tolerance 138
Put-down Survey 141

A Fold Apart 144
The Classroom Tree 146
What Are My Roots? 148
Good or Bad? Teaching Ethics 149
Taking Control of Anger 153
Chart Your Anger! 156
Scary Stories 158
On the Fear Line! 161
Crises Happen! 164
Dealing with Crisis 166

Welcome to Counselor in the Classroom

Effective counseling can have a powerful impact on the ability of all students to learn, and to manage themselves in the classroom, the school, and all other areas of their lives. As counselors, we hold the keys to some of the most vital, sought-after, life-skills that people of any age can develop. In a lifetime, many individuals never acquire these skills, yet we have the power to teach them to children! Not just the children who are referred to us, but all children.

Counselors can help students feel comfortable in the school environment, develop positive self-concepts, and rediscover the motivation to learn. We have the ability to enhance open communication and promote cooperative work skills. We can create a renaissance in interpersonal relations by developing listening, speaking, and observation skills, and promoting tolerance and the ability of young people to get along well with others.

In addition to training in life-skills, counselors can help students make continuous links between classroom learning and the career futures that await them, and prepare students to deal with change. We can show students the path of responsibility, teaching them to be safe, to resist substance abuse, and to shun violence and bullying. Through our efforts students can develop an entire repertoire of skills associated with problem-solving, decision-making, assertiveness, and conflict resolution.

These keys—the skills and abilities that counselors possess—are essential for the success of the entire learning community, not just students. They benefit teachers, administrators, parents, support staff, and every other individual or group that interfaces with schools.

So why aren't parents demanding that schools hire more counselors? Why aren't employers lobbying school board members to put greater emphasis on life-skills, and why aren't administrators asking teams of counselors to create systematic, developmental guidance curriculums? Because, in schools, learning has taken place in the classroom—the domain of the teacher —but counselors are now forging the cooperative relationships necessary to enter that domain on a regular, systematic basis and to become a part of it.

Counselor in the Classroom is a way to do this. It offers a collection of learning activities designed to optimally utilize the skills of counselors and bring those skills into the classroom.

A New Perception

A profound change has occurred among counselors. After sitting for decades in offices seeing only those children who were referred due to problems or who were assertive enough to demand services, we have finally determined that counseling is for all students.

How is counseling delivered to all students? With the help of a vehicle called *Instructional Guidance*. *Counselor in the Classroom* is a manifestation of instructional guidance—a healthy slice of guidance curriculum designed to be delivered to classroom-size groups.

The new focus is pro-active, rather than reactive. It is preventive rather than crisis oriented. Guidance curricula are designed to help all students develop personal, educational, social, and career skills, and to become responsible and productive citizens. They take the form of systematic programs in which all students are involved, and they necessitate working with groups rather than solely with individuals.

An Old Reality

As counselors we have turned the corner, and we know how things "ought to be." Many of us are willing and able to serve as consultants in the classroom. *Counselor in the Classroom* is a welcome tool. However, in planning our classroom presence, we have to understand the reality we're facing. What can we expect of students, what are the constraints of teachers, and how are most counselors still perceived?

Media Kids

The student population is highly diverse. This diversity extends far beyond race, ethnicity, and culture. Students bring widely varying levels of readiness to the classroom. Some are gifted, enthusiastic learners, others are sedated by television and other media, still others get too little sleep, and a few have come to believe that violence is an appropriate way to deal with conflict.

Today, media is one of the most pervasive of influences. Its engaging audio and visual images captivate not just the attention, but the thinking of children. It has become the great informal educator of our youth. Research tells us that too much media of any type retards the development of oral-language skills (Who talks with a media device?). In the "sound bite" language modeled by television, YouTube, and other media fragmented ideas or expressions are completed with visual images, making the need for fluent verbal expression unnecessary. These use a combination of auditory and visual cues to make a statement. Since students can't use similarly elaborate visual images to supplement their words, inadequate oral language skills render significant numbers functionally disabled in the area of language. Classrooms and teachers have inherited the daunting task of not only teaching oral-language skills but countering the deleterious effects of the world outside of school. Modeling good communication and facilitating effective dialogue among students is even more difficult in overcrowded classrooms.

If retarding the development of oral language skills isn't enough, most media demonstrates another ability. Because their visual images leave so little to the imagination, students are not required to think about what they are seeing. Instead they simply react. Research tells us that when people react favorably and without thought, they tend to become addicted to the stimulus that produces the favorable reaction. In the case of some media (games in particular), the addiction is not just to the programming but to the act of watching or looking and participating. (Recall times when you or a companion flipped through the TV channels, looking but never really enjoying a program from beginning to end.)

When we rely on such complete and vivid visual portrayals, our brain stops engaging a particular operation critical to thinking and learning. This operation is known as the implicit thinking mechanism. It's the device our brain uses to connect random knowledge to practical application.

Authentic assessment models tell us that children are having difficulty connecting facts they are given to practical uses in their lives. What they've lost is the ability to imagine, and with it the ability to solve problems and see relevance to what they learn. Additionally, the dramatic content of some media is condensed into very short time segments. Children observe weeks, months, and sometimes years of living compressed into a few minutes of media engagement. This has the effect of destroying the concept of delayed gratification which is at the root of effective self-management.

Finally, media, clearly and with staggering repetition, dispenses a flow of situations in which violence is shown as an appropriate strategy for resolving conflict (even the "good guys" use it).

All of these factors find their way into today's classroom. Given the enormous stresses children experience both in and out of school, it is little wonder that the classroom is such a challenging place to be.

The Constraints of Teachers

Teachers today are working with children who present a whole host of new challenges to teaching and learning—children who bring with them to school unprecedented levels of sophistication, both good and bad. In many schools, discipline and self-management have become critical concerns, their relative absence among students posing severe threats to teaching and learning.

These breakdowns coupled with large class sizes have required an increasing focus on classroom management (often confused with discipline) to the depletion of valuable teaching time. Good management and good teaching are mutually exclusive activities. When a teacher engages in one, she or he does so at the expense of the other. What we need is more good teaching, but what we're getting are teachers who devote more, not less, time to classroom management.

Dictates imposed by the curriculum and classroom procedures are two other continuing realities for teachers. Mandated programs for the classroom very often meet with natural resistance because of their intrusive qualities. They can be both professionally and personally disruptive and upsetting to teachers. Some of these programs are highly prescriptive. Lock-step programs take away teacher initiative and erode feelings of professionalism. The teacher begins to perceive the classroom as constrictive and lacking room for creativity and innovation.

Given the emphasis on authentic assessment for students, it is surprising that attention is just now being given to this type of assessment for teachers and other school personnel. Teacher evaluations have always been heavily subjective. This reality further compounds the dilemma of teachers as they try to balance their attention between what's good for children with what's good for themselves. Very often, the criteria used to evaluate teachers have little or nothing to do with the quality of the learning experience for children.

An extension of this reality has to do with the idea of "teaching to tests." When teachers are caught between their own subjective evaluations and being compelled to prepare students for tests that don't effectively measure learning, they experience another dimension of professional distress.

Health officials report that classroom teaching is among the most stressful professions. Stress in teaching arises largely from the demands we place on teachers and the degree to which teachers have become isolated in the school setting. Teachers have little opportunity to enjoy fulfilling collegiality and consequently are at substantial mental and physical risk.

When health risks are considered along with the other challenges outlined, classroom teaching is a tough business to be in. And if that's not enough, teachers today face a dangerous new reality in the form of the physical violence perpetrated in schools. The incidence of assaults on teachers is rising at an alarming rate and shows no sign of declining. Taken together, these factors portray the current reality of classroom teaching as challenging indeed.

How Counselors Are (Still) Viewed

One of the most significant realities currently existing in education is the pervasive misunderstanding of the role of school counselors. Events have shaped an educational policy that can undervalue counselors and underestimate their potential. The enormous stresses weighing on public education have in many cases relegated the counselor to a position roughly equivalent to adjunct administrator, firefighters, and crisis manager combined.

In the order of things, counselors are often among the first to go when districts are faced with reductions in force. Even worse, in an expanding climate of restructuring and reform, counselors and counseling are sometimes not perceived as having a role.

When asked, counselors report that client load and paperwork are the greatest impediments to their effectiveness. This is true, but also true is the fact that these impediments reflect the perception, role, and value given to counselors and counseling by school boards and administrators. Counselors are too often seen as administrative adjuncts, not vital contributors to student success. Though changing, many school superintendents, building principals, teachers, and parents don't understand what the role of counseling is, and others don't value the role they understand. School counselors and counseling have been in the shadows— credited with neither their contributions nor their potential to contribute.

Too few counselor resources (too few counselors and too little support) have created a reality that has jeopardized both counselors and counseling. In the context of schools where classrooms are overcrowded and the frequency of student referrals grows daily, counselors are professionally challenged as never before, and need to be incorporated into proposed solutions.

All over the country, school districts, state education departments, and legislatures continue creating school reform. Virtually every reform initiative is front loaded with a call for not only higher and more highly validated academic achievement, but substantial social and emotional development— the very things counselors have been trained to deliver.

The Learning Community

The learning community represents all the stakeholders in education. It includes teachers, students, administrators, counselors, parents, support staff, business, community-based organizations, public agencies, unions, and more. The learning community is deep and broad and is being depended upon to perform.

In a culture where we hear words like quality and performance almost every day in one context or another, consider these words of the noted author and speaker Dr. Denis Waitley: "Performance is a reflection not a measure of quality. Performance can't wait for measurement." It is in this spirit that we have drawn from the current reality an opportunity to move from the shadows into the light. We perceive—and wish others to perceive— counselors as vital contributors to the classroom and in turn to student performance. We perceive counselors as enhancers of the quality of the teaching experience for teachers themselves.

All of us are driven by a desire to be, and be seen as, successful. When any of us is perceived as contributing significantly to the success of others, resources flow to us. Therefore, when counselors are perceived as vital to classroom and teacher success and, in turn, to the success of the school and district, counselor resources are likely to grow.

Linking Counseling to Outcomes

Counselors and teachers are natural allies—each has much to contribute to the other. Counselors in classrooms can have a positive influence on learning outcomes by addressing areas outside the core curriculum that directly impinge upon student performance.

Stress Management

Today, students are experiencing high levels of stress on a regular basis. Indeed, some mental health experts maintain that unmanaged distress is the greatest deterrent to learning in American education. Under high levels of stress, students experience a deterioration in their ability to think and learn. Research indicates that the cognitive mechanisms of the brain/mind complex shut down in direct proportion to the amount of distress experienced. These mechanisms are essential to comprehension and reasoning. In their absence, students cannot learn regardless of the skill of the teacher.

At the same time, teachers are experiencing greater stress, too—job stresses that affect physical and mental health, reduce teaching effectiveness, and significantly lower enjoyment, motivation, and personal job satisfaction.

Anything that can be done to help teachers and students learn to manage stress and the situations in their lives that produce it can have a profound and measurable effect on learning and achievement. Since both learning and achievement are clearly "in the light," any intervention that enhances them will be perceived by all concerned as having significant value.

And stress management is within the domain of the counselor.

Conflict Management

Among the most stressful events in our lives are those involving conflict. Conflict in the classroom disrupts teaching and places additional demands on classroom management. A simple conflict in class, when poorly managed, can destroy an entire period or a significant part of the teaching day and, in turn, negatively impact learning.

An important understanding for students and teachers alike is that conflict is a normal part of living—neither good nor bad—and that the *consequences* of conflict are what cause us to see it as good or bad. Students who learn to manage conflicts effectively can and do produce positive results.

And teaching the skills of conflict management is within the domain of the counselor.

Communication Skills

Few skills have greater and more lasting value to students than the ability to listen. Unfortunately, listening skills are generally learned by happenstance, not by direct effort, and the results are predictable: the vast majority of adults and children in this country are either unable or unwilling to listen attentively and at length to another person.

Research indicates that deficient listening impedes learning and destroys comprehension. However, when students are taught to listen effectively, we not only find that comprehension and academic performance go up, we also observe greater classroom cooperation and enhanced self-esteem. Needless to say, comprehension, performance, cooperation, and self-esteem are highly valued by educators in general and by teachers in particular.

And listening along with other elements of good communication is within the domain of the counselor.

And the List Goes On...

Creative and critical thinking skills form the underpinnings of problem-solving and decision-making, processes that are crucial to learning and growth and clearly fall within the domain of the counselor.

The ability to set goals enables students to establish challenging yet realistic targets for academic achievement and also falls within the domain of the counselor.

A review of the table of contents may broaden your vision of what you can offer students and teachers in the classroom setting. For example, you are the appropriate person to address self-esteem, tolerance, bullying, peer pressure, attitude, conduct, personal safety, test anxiety, and ethics. All of these topics are within your domain.

As teachers come to view counselors and counseling as integral parts of their own success, they become outspoken advocates for counseling. They understand that the role we play is indispensable to their performance as, indeed, it should be.

Counselor-Driven Learnings

Virtually all of our knowledge and skills are learned incrementally. It's the accumulation over time of bits and pieces of learning that added together produce everything we know and understand.

Traditional approaches to teaching in schools utilize a particular kind of incremental learning called "focused incremental learning." In focused incremental learning, content is segmented across a scope and sequence directed at producing particular learning outcomes (the focus). Virtually every part of core curriculum and most other courses of study use this focused approach.

However, among all the things we learn, or stand to learn, the great majority are assimilated through a different kind of incremental learning known as "random incremental learning." Random incremental learnings are produced from all the accumulated experiences we have that are associated with something we perceive as valuable to us. Lacking scope or sequence, these learnings enter our lives randomly, some by chance and others by choice. Either way, they are rarely part of a directed course of study with specified outcomes.

When random learnings are elevated to the status of focused learnings, we find that more can be taught in less time (some random learnings take a lifetime to acquire). When we apply quality learning and teaching strategies to this process, we produce outstanding results. In the area of linguistics, for example, new methods of producing focused learnings have proven very successful. Integrated and interdisciplinary approaches to curriculum have generated similar results. Impressive innovations are occurring in technology education and in the use of manipulatives as well. All of this is good news.

The bad news is that virtually every learning area that falls within the counselor's domain is still left to random learning. One of the goals of *Counselor in the Classroom* is to help us raise all of these areas to the status of focused learning through the use of an instructional guidance program. With a systematic, sequential guidance curriculum in hand, we can position ourselves as vital classroom resources.

The *Counselor in the Classroom* Approach

Each set of activities in *Counselor in the Classroom* offers us valuable ways to respond to the needs of our teacher colleagues. More than this, each set can be a jumping-off point for an expanded thematic unit that we and our teacher colleagues can cooperatively integrate into the classroom. Instructional guidance is not a separate and supplementary service, but rather an essential ingredient in the classroom mix, integrated into daily lessons. Separating the guidance curriculum from teaching neglects the role of the teacher in the guidance process and fails to take full advantage of the services that counselors bring to the learning process and to teacher-student relations.

Counselors and teachers are beginning to cooperate to ensure that all students benefit from counseling and guidance, not just those who are referred or dealt with on an exceptional basis. We can take advantage of this move toward collaboration, this marriage of opportunity, by giving ourselves and our programs a clear identity and winning the support of our teacher colleagues.

To do this, we must introduce the idea of integrating counseling and guidance with instruction, and persuade teachers that this collaboration serves everyone, representing the best in education for all concerned. An integrated approach is based on the belief that successful teaching focuses on the whole child, and on every child.

Teachers are challenged in their roles. As a counselor in the classroom, our job is to help teachers fully meet that challenge. Our understanding of human development and social/emotional growth is essential to the promotion of higher levels of classroom success for teachers and students alike.

The *Counselor in the Classroom* approach is to have every school counselor become a vital ingredient in the success of every teacher with whom he or she works. This book is a response to the many counselors who have expressed a need for a guidance curriculum that can be used in a classroom setting.

How to Use Counselor in the Classroom

Let Your Skills Shine Through

One of the joys of writing a curriculum for counselors is knowing that some of the most powerful skills for facilitating learning are already part of the counselor's repertoire and will be applied expertly.

During class discussions, your listening skills are your strength, and your ability to reflect, clarify, and summarize will be tremendously facilitating. Model these skills for students and teachers alike. At the same time, take full advantage of the outstanding teachers with whom you work. Ask for pointers relative to instructional techniques and try out the suggestions you receive. By observing teachers, you can perfect your presentation and large-group skills.

Sequence and Variation

The activities in *Counselor in the Classroom* are grouped into topic areas and arranged in a suggested developmental sequence. However, the current arrangement allows for a great deal of flexibility. Feel free to move about the book freely, gearing your choices to the specific needs or interest areas of students and teachers. Do try to lead an introductory activity first; and do build a base of intrapersonal and interpersonal skills early. These will serve you and the students well when more challenging topics are addressed.

How Often and How Long

In developing cooperative, team relationships with the teachers at your school, you will need to negotiate time on a case by case basis. One hour-long visit a week might be a good place to start. (Most of the activities in *Counselor in the Classroom* can be implemented in less than 60 minutes.) If you and a teacher hit it off exceptionally well, add more visits. If a teacher shows signs of feeling crowded or disrupted, back off.

Even if you are working regularly in several classrooms over the course of a semester or term, you are not likely to run out of activities. The only person who will have to deal with repetition is you, and with each use your ability to deliver a particular activity will be enhanced.

Maintain an Expansive, Flexible Attitude

As you lead activities, make presentations, and facilitate discussions, the direct and indirect feedback you receive from students and teachers will doubtless spark many ideas for additional lessons in particular topic areas. Be sure to keep a written record of these ideas so that you can expand and refine your guidance curriculum.

Adjust for the Ages and Interests of Students

Many activities in *Counselor in the Classroom* include suggestions concerning simplified versions for younger students, or other modifications. If you have doubts about the readiness of a class for a particular concept or type of activity, consult with the teacher ahead of time. (Actually, you might want to do this as a matter of course with all teachers.) The teacher's instructional expertise and familiarity with the students will sometimes generate extremely valuable alternative approaches. Try them.

Collaborate!

As a counselor, you've been exposed to numerous resources and ideas that will be helpful in delivering guidance activities. Because teachers are so busy preparing academic lessons, they will appreciate any assistance you can give them in locating appropriate resources and materials. For this reason, *Counselor in the Classroom* includes a number of supplemental activities for teachers.

In addition, many activities include follow-up sessions. Some follow-ups may be facilitated by the teacher and are so indicated; others require your presence and continued leadership. If you are visiting a class weekly or more often, follow-ups will rarely be a problem. If you are visiting less frequently, follow-ups will have to be negotiated on a per-activity basis.

Teachers should remain in class to either participate along with students, or observe and assist as you lead the guidance activity. From their observations, teachers will be able to plan follow-up instruction. These collaborative efforts also allow teachers and counselors to exchange constructive feedback that will be helpful in planning future guidance activities and services for individual students.

Publicize Your Availability

Let teachers know about your expanding role so that they can help you carve a long-term, renewable niche for instructional guidance within the existing curriculum. Give teachers a list of topic areas so they'll realize that you can assist with the development of such vital competencies as decision-making, goal-setting, communication, personal management, conflict management, and safety skills.

Hold an inservice to acquaint teachers with your instructional guidance curriculum. Allow them to experience selected activities themselves, and solicit their feedback and cooperation.

Consider Yourself Precious

Most schools have many classrooms and one or a handful of counselors. You are a priceless package of skills and resources. You are a person who can be depended upon to make children feel good about themselves, to bring comfort, to generate warmth, to develop life skills, and to teach important lessons about living.

Go easy on yourself. If an activity doesn't produce the desired results the first time you lead it, get some feedback from the teacher, modify the activity, and try it again with another class. If you've never been a polished presenter, don't worry. While you hone your presentation skills, know that the skills you do possess—listening, facilitating, sharing insights—are more important anyway.

Be yourself. Be the counselor. Be the counselor in the classroom! ...and enjoy!

- **Counselor and Teacher Activities**

- **Student Experience Sheets**

Who is the Counselor?

An Introductory Counselor Activity

Overall Purpose:

To focus your initial visit to the classroom on the special role you play at school and the services you offer students, their families, and staff. An Experience Sheet helps generate student involvement and interaction in this process, and a "take-home" letter ensures that parents too are informed of your presence and availability.

Materials:

One copy of the Student Experience Sheet, *Who Sees the Counselor?*, for each student; copies of the take-home letter, "Introducing the Counselor" for the teacher to distribute to students at the end of the day.

Directions:

Introduce yourself to the students (or ask the teacher to introduce you). Tell the children where your office is located, what your hours are, and paint a verbal picture of what you do. For example, briefly describe your activities on a typical day.

Next, distribute the Experience Sheet, *Who Sees the Counselor?* Go over the directions and give the students a few minutes to read the sheet and complete it.

While the students are working, write on the board the names of the youthful characters pictured on the experience sheet (Maria, Billy, Joan, Manuel, Kim, David, and Donna.) When the students have finished, point to each name in turn and ask:

How many think that the counselor would be pleased to see and talk with (Maria)?

Count the hands that are raised and write the total on the board.

When you are finished going through the list, tell the children that they are *all right* — because a counselor would be pleased to see every one of the children pictured.

Go back through the list and briefly explain what a counselor might do to help each child. Give examples from your own experience and emphasize throughout that you are the person who does these things at your school.

Conclude the activity with a general discussion, using the questions listed below or others that you think of.

Discussion Questions:

1. What are some reasons that you or your classmates might want to see the counselor?
2. Why is it important to find someone to talk to when you have a problem?
3. Can you think of a reason you might want to talk with the counselor that does not involve a problem?
4. If you wanted to talk with the counselor, how would you go about it? What would you do first? ...second? ...third?

Variations:

If you are working with beginning or non-readers, do not distribute the experience sheet. Instead, read aloud one item at a time from the sheet and ask for a show of hands after each example. Write totals on the board and complete the remainder of the activity as written.

Who Sees the Counselor?

Student Experience Sheet

Which of the students below would the counselor be happy to see? Circle any that you think should go to the counselor.

Billy lost his house key and his parents won't be home from work until after dark.

Joan has a disability that makes her talk differently from the other kids. Some kids tease her and don't include her in groups. This makes Joan very unhappy.

David is new at school. He feels lonely and shy.

Kim got an A on her Math test. She wants to tell someone about it.

Manuel built a great computer-controlled robot at home. He wants to know if he can enter it in the district science fair.

Maria is worried because her parents are getting a divorce. She wishes someone could understand her sad feelings.

Donna has been getting low grades on tests. She's having trouble studying at home.

Use this sample letter. *Fill in the name of the class (e.g., "Mr. Robert's 4th grade class") at the top along with your name and title. At the bottom, write your name and phone number. Make any other changes you wish and reproduce!*

To: All Students and Parents of _____
From: _____

Introducing, the Counselor!

A counselor is someone who listens and doesn't judge how you speak, or what you say, or what you're feeling. A counselor tells the truth, and keeps a secret.

A counselor is special because he or she listens when you're feeling lonely, sad, or mad. When something worries you so much that you can't really talk about it to anyone. When you're frightened, confused, or down, or put-down. When school doesn't seem to be working out, or you're getting in fights.

I am a counselor. I'm here for you. I'm here for your family, too. If you need me, all you have to do is let me know. Leave me a note in the principal's office, or tell your teacher you'd like to see me. We'll talk a little bit, or maybe just take a walk together, and see what happens. That's about all. It's simple and easy.

My name is _____ , and you can call me at, _____ , or you can leave a note in my mailbox in the school office. I'd like to get to know you better.

Validations
A Counselor Activity

Overall Purpose:

You are in an ideal position to help students learn to appreciate themselves and others. Use the safe, game-like format of this activity to show students how to make deliberate, positive comments to others.

Materials:

8 1/2 X 11 blank paper, fine-point marking pens in dark colors (one per student), and masking tape

Directions:

Announce that today your mission is to help create *validations* for everyone.

Ask if anyone knows what a validation is — or what it means to validate someone. Listen to all responses; if you like, jot ideas on the board. Explain that a validation is an expression of approval, and that to validate someone means to say something positive that lets that person know you respect and appreciate him or her.

Make these additional points about validations:
- A validation is similar to a compliment. *I like the way you fixed your hair today* and *I think you're nice to help me with my math proble* are validations.
- Receiving validations from others feels good and builds our self-esteem.
- Giving a validation is like giving a gift, and it doesn't cost a penny.
- Validations should always be sincere. Usually people can tell when we say something we don't really mean.
- At first it may feel strange to give validations, but with practice anyone can do it.

- A validation expresses what you are thinking and feeling, so try starting it with the word "I." (I think..., ...feel, ...appreciate, ...like, etc.)
- Be as clear and specific as you can. Describe what you like or appreciate in the other person. If you say, *You're fun*, or, *You look nice*. the person won't understand nearly as well as if you say, *I love the clever things you say*, or *I really like you in that red shirt*.

Ask the students to help you formulate different kinds of validations. Keep coming up with examples until you're reasonably sure the students have a good grasp of the concept.

Give each student a sheet of paper, a marking pen, and a couple of pieces of masking tape. Have the students help each other tape the papers to their backs. Then, in your own words, give these directions:

We're going to practice giving each other validations. I want everyone to get up and start walking around the room. Think of something positive and sincere to communicate to each person you meet. But instead of saying the words, use your pen to write the words on the person's back. Keep it brief and write in small letters, because I want each of you to write something on the back of every person in the room.

Circulate and monitor the students to make sure that they write only positive statements. When they have finished, give the students a minute or two to remove the papers from their backs and read the comments that people have written. Then lead a brief culminating discussion.

Discussion Questions:

1. How does it feel to validate others?
2. How does it feel to be validated?
3. Which of the comments on your back surprised you?
4. What are some other ways to show people that you appreciate them?

Variations:

Simplify the explanation for children in lower grades, giving lots of examples of simple *I like your (smile, friendship, shoes, hair, etc.)* statements. Then, as they roam around the room, have the children deliver their positive statements to each other orally. If the class is large, limit the number of children on the floor at any one time, completing the exercise in perhaps three rounds. Don't attempt to have every child compliment every other child.

Images of Me
An Counselor Activity

Overall Purpose:

This activity builds and reinforces positive self-images and self-esteem very directly, by allowing the students to graphically represent three different self-images, viewing and talking about the significance of each and the feelings they engender.

Materials:

Multiple copies of three or more large shapes (circle, triangle, rectangle, etc.) cut from colored construction paper; large sheets of white poster board or construction paper; colored markers, crayons, scissors, and glue.

Directions:

Introduce the concept of self-image. Explain that an image is a picture of something. It can be a photograph or drawing, but it can also be the image we see in our mind when we think of the real thing. Self-image is how we mentally see ourselves.

In your own words, explain further:

Each of us may have several different self-images. You may have one image when you think of yourself at home with your family, and a very different one when you think of yourself playing baseball with your friends. Today, I want you to think of three of the best images you have of yourself and draw them. Then, you'll use those three drawings to design a poster all about you.

Give each student three different construction-paper shapes, and ask a couple of students to distribute scissors, markers/crayons, glue, and poster board. While the students are getting set up, write the following list on the board:

>
> My Family and Me
> Me and My Friends
> A Favorite Place
> A Favorite Possession
> My Pet and Me
> A Favorite Day of the Year
> A Dream Vacation
> A Favorite Game or Sport
> My Best School Subject
> Something I'm Proud Of

Read through the list with the students, and explain:

Choose any topic from the list, and write the topic at the top of one of your shapes. Draw a picture on that shape, showing the image you have in your mind when you think of that topic. Then, choose two more topics and label and illustrate your other two shapes. When you have finished all three, move the shapes around on a sheet of poster board until you come up with a design that you like. Finally, glue the shapes in place. Title your poster, Images of (your name).

Circulate during the work phase of the activity, and engage the students in brief conversations about their pictures. Arrange to have the teacher display the posters around the room, or borrow them for a few days, displaying them on walls or bulletin boards near your office.

Before you leave, go around the room and have every student hold up his or her poster and briefly describe what's happening in each of the three pictures. Facilitate a culminating discussion about the importance of having positive self-images.

Discussion Questions:

1. When you imagine yourself in a positive picture, how do you feel?
2. When your image of yourself is poor, how do you feel?
3. Where do we get the images we have of ourselves?
4. Why is it important to see ourselves in positive ways?

Variations:

Provide several patterns, and have the students cut out their own shapes, or have them trace around the patterns to make the images directly on their poster board.

When working with young children, read through the list of topics several times. Then circulate and assist with labeling shapes and titling posters.

Feeling Faces
A Counselor Activity

Overall Purpose:

Use this activity to help students identify a variety of feelings and associate them with feeling words, and to provide opportunities for students to recall and share incidents in which they experienced various feelings.

Materials:

Paper plates, flat wooden sticks (such as tongue depressors or popsicle sticks), scissors, colored markers and/or crayons, and glue

Directions:

Get the attention of the students and tell them to listen carefully while you read them the poem/story below. Ask the students to listen for feelings and to remember as many as they can.

> Angry at Marty
> Loving t'ward Lou
> I'm full of feelings
> What shall I do?
>
> Proud of my drawing
> Jealous of your bike
> I show my feelings
> And hide them, too
>
> Happy after winning
> Sad when I lose
> I change my feelings
> Like I change my shoes.

Tired in the morning
Hungry at noon
Do you have feelings
That bother you, too?

Depressed by grades
Scared of the dark
Why all these feelings...
What good do they do?

Surprised by mysteries
Amused by cartoons
If you lack feelings
I'll give some to you.

Excited by birthdays
Bored when they're through
I'll understand feelings
In a year or two.

After you have read the poem, ask the students to call out the feeling words that they identified. Point out that it is perfectly normal to experience all of the feelings mentioned and that, while everyone experiences them, each person feels and expresses them a little differently. Jot each word on the board and add others until you have a list that includes:

happy	sad	scared
angry	proud	excited
confused	tired	surprised
bored	amused	jealous
loving	hungry	depressed

Have the students pair up. Distribute the mask-making materials and, in your own words, explain:

You are going to work together to create a mask that shows one of the feelings listed on the board. First, agree on the feeling you want to illustrate and then, using colored markers, make a face on the paper plate that depicts that feeling. Exaggerate the features to make the feeling come across as forcefully as possible.

Demonstrate the process, or show the students a mask that you have made in advance. Circulate and help the students cut eye holes in their masks and glue their sticks in place to create handles.

When the masks are finished, have each pair join three other pairs to form circles of eight. Direct the students to take turns holding their mask in front of their face, relating a time when they experienced the feeling shown, and acting out some of the things they did and said to express that feeling. Have the teacher circulate with you and coach the students, as necessary, reminding them to pass their mask to their partner after they have had a turn.

Suggest that the masks be displayed around the room and that the students continue to use them throughout the year to aid them in expressing feelings. Conclude the activity with a total group discussion.

Discussion Questions:

1. Which feelings were easiest to express and recognize? Which were hardest? Why do you think that is?
2. How did you feel when you were acting out your situation?
3. Did the mask make it easier to act out your feelings? Why or why not?
4. Why is it important to be aware of and express our feelings?
5. Who decided how you would express your feeling? In real life, who always decides?
6. When you have feelings that make it hard for you to work in school, what can you do to feel better? Whom can you talk to?

Variations:

- Make paper-bag masks, which require large eye holes but no gluing.
- If the group is relatively small, lead the sharing, dramatizations, and discussion in one large circle.
- If time is short, spread the activity over two visits. Make the masks during the first visit; lead the sharing, dramatizations, and discussion during the second visit.

The Ups and Downs of Feelings

A Counselor Activity

Overall Purpose:

This activity is designed to help students identify a number of feelings, and link them with specific events in their lives. The students are encouraged to take responsibility for negative feelings by engaging in activities that relieve stress and build positive energy.

Materials:

One copy of the experience sheet, *The Roller Coaster Ride of Life* for each student

Directions:

When you greet the students, ask them how they are. If someone says, *fine* or *great*, ask: *Does "fine" mean that you're having a good day? What's causing you to feel good?*

Initiate a discussion about how different events — and our thoughts about those events — cause us to have various feelings. Give several examples, and elicit others from the group.

Draw a roller-coaster line on the board. Trace the peaks and valleys with your finger (to illustrate) as you introduce the roller-coaster analogy. In your own words, say:

Life is similar to a roller-coaster ride. When good things happen, we go shooting up to the highest points and we feel elated and joyful. When not-so-good things happen, we start coming down again. We may feel uncertain, confused, or unhappy. Certain events take us all the way to the bottom, where we experience grief and anger. When that happens, we have to build up lots of energy in order to climb to the top again.

Distribute the experience sheets, and tell the students that you want them to take a few minutes to think about the highs and lows on their own "roller coaster ride." Go over the directions; then give the students about 10 minutes to complete the sheet. While they are working, label the roller coaster on the board with three "high" events and three "low" events from your own experience.

When the students have finished, share with them your own events (from the board). Then have them share what they have written in groups of four or five. In a culminating discussion, talk about the need to accept all feelings, whether pleasant or unpleasant. Focus on ways of building or renewing energy during low points.

Discussion Questions:

1. Do you know of any roller coasters with tracks that are flat and even? Do you think such a roller coaster would be fun?
2. Do you think it's possible to never feel sad or angry? Why or why not?
3. How do your thoughts about an event cause you to have certain feelings?
4. If you could control your thoughts, how do you think it would affect your feelings?
5. Why is it important to "let off steam" when we feel angry or sad?
6. Who is in control of your feelings? ...of your thoughts?

The Roller-Coaster Ride of Life

Student Experience Sheet

Life sure has ups and downs, doesn't it? Some times your feelings lift you way up, and sometimes they drag you way down. The ride of life is a lot like a roller coaster ride.

It's normal to feel bad when you're down. What are some of your lowest lows? Pick two from this list, or think of others. Then go to the next page and write them on the lines below the roller coaster. Write three of your highest highs on the lines at the top of the roller coaster.

HIGHS
When:
—you get a new pet
—you make a new friend.
—you take a trip or vacation
—you get an "A"
—your parents are in a great mood
—someone really listens to you
—you look your best
—you're having fun with friends
—you buy something new
—your team wins
—you feel confident about an assignment or task

LOWS
When:
—your pet is lost or dies
—a friend moves away
—you move away from friends
—you get a bad grade on a test
—your parents argue
—no one seems to understand you
—you think you're unattractive
—there's nothing to do and no one to play with
—you don't have enough money to do something you really want to do
—you lose a game or contest
—you don't feel capable of doing an assignment or task

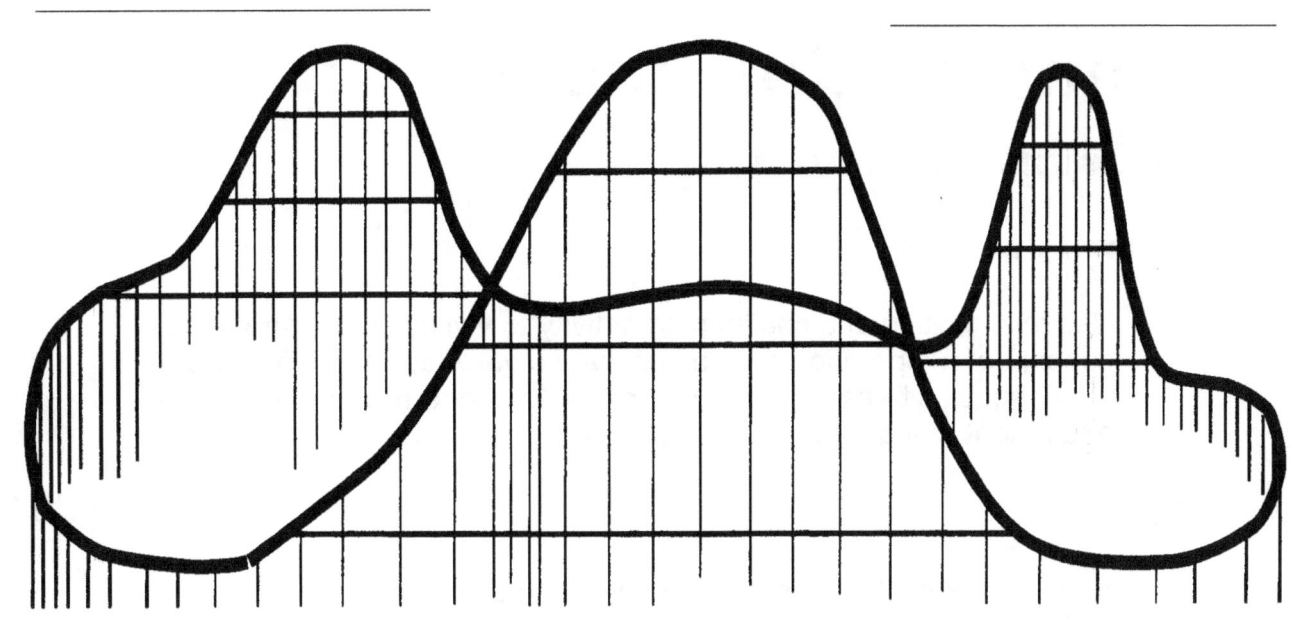

When you feel low, try not to sit around feeling sorry for yourself. Do something to get rid of those bad feelings. Here are some ideas. Write two of your favorite activities on the blank lines.

1. Talk to someone who cares.

2. Go for a bike ride, walk, or jog.

3. Write about your feelings in your diary or journal.

4. Read a book, watch a video, or play a computer game.

5. Play with your pet.

6. Bake a cake or cookies.

7. Draw, paint, sew, sculpt, or design.

8. Pull weeds or fix something that's broken.

9. Listen to music, or play an instrument.

10. Rearrange your room.

11. _____

12. _____

Construction Teams

A Counselor Activity

Overall Purpose:

Use this exciting and challenging activity to vividly demonstrate the concept of cooperation and to generate awareness and discussion about specific behaviors that contribute to cooperative goal attainment in a group.

Materials:

Several boxes of straws, extra long match sticks (with the heads broken off), popsicle sticks, or other construction materials; one role of transparent tape for each small group

Directions:

Divide the students into groups of five or six. Distribute the materials. Tell the students that they are going to play a game in which each group is a construction team whose members work together to build a structure with the materials you have provided. They may build a house, bridge, tower, spacecraft, dome, or any other structure. However, since this is a game, there are rules. Explain the rules as follows:

- *Everyone is to be involved.*
- *Team members will have 1 minute to talk among themselves and decide on a type of structure to build.*
- *When I tell you to start building your structures, you must stop talking and remain silent until the end of the game.*
- *You may communicate with each other nonverbally — with gestures, facial expressions, etc. but no words.*
- *All teams will start with 50 points.*
- *Teams will lose 2 points each time a member talks.*
- *Teams will have 15 minutes to build their structures.*

While the students take a minute to plan their structure, draw a simple score chart on the board, numbering or naming each team.

Then start the game. Circulate and observe the groups, noting the effectiveness of nonverbal communication, the degree of inclusion and cooperation, who the leaders are in each group, and any drop-outs (students who are either ignored by their team or choose not to become involved). Calculate talking infractions on the score chart.

After 15 minutes, call time. Point out the scores on the board and congratulate all of the teams, giving special recognition to the team with the highest score.

One at a time, have the teams show and explain their structure to the class, and evaluate themselves based on these questions:
— *How well did you cooperate and work together?*
— *Did one or two team members do most of the work, or was everyone involved?*
— *What was your communication like?*
— *Did you accomplish your goal?*
— *How satisfied are you with your structure?*
— *Were there any conflicts in the group and how did you handle them?*
— *What did you do about members who talked?*

Contribute observations of your own, as appropriate. After every team has had an opportunity to share, lead a culminating discussion, focusing on the importance of cooperating with others.

Discussion Questions:

1. What is the meaning of the word cooperation?
2. Why is cooperation important when people work together?
3. What kinds of things happen when people don't cooperate?
4. What specific things did you do in your group that demonstrated cooperation?
5. If you were to play the game again, what could you do to improve your cooperation?

Variations:

Have one person on each team be an observer. Take the observers aside before the game starts and tell them what to watch for. Then, after the game, have the observers give feedback to their team.

Pictures Speak Words
A Counselor Activity

Overall Purpose:

This activity gives students an opportunity to evaluate their own behaviors in a team situation, and to gain experiential knowledge of the importance of cooperation.

Materials:

Words or phrases written on individual slips of paper (see below); clock or watch with second hand; chart paper and colored markers

Directions:

Before visiting the class, work with the teacher to determine what words or phrases you want to use in the game. Choose words that are related to lessons you or the teacher have already taught in the class, or to a theme you want to focus on during this visit. For example, words drawn from key activities in this curriculum are *cooperation, teamwork, communication, friendship, self-esteem, and peer pressure.* You might also choose words related to an upcoming holiday, or words on a recent vocabulary list obtained from the teacher. Write each word or phrase on a slip of paper.

Explain to the students that they are going to play a game very much like Pictionary. Divide the class into teams of six to ten. (Traditionally this game is played by two teams, but there is no reason why you cannot create more.) Then explain the rules/procedures of the game:

When it is your team's turn, one member chooses a slip of paper and tries to communicate to his or her teammates the word written on the paper. This person <u>may not talk</u>, but may draw pictures and symbols on the board (or chart) as clues. The team, which <u>may</u> talk and ask questions, tries to guess the word. Questions may not be answered verbally, only with gestures or more pictures and symbols. However, when the team correctly guesses a letter or portion of the word or phrase, the person who is "it" may write those letters on the board. You will have 3 minutes to guess the word; if you succeed, you win 1 point. If you do not guess correctly, the other team(s) has one chance to guess the word and wins a point if it succeeds. Then it is another team's turn.

Start the game, and serve as timekeeper and scorekeeper. Play for as long as time allows or until you have exhausted your supply of words/phrases (making sure that all teams have an equal number of opportunities to score points). Then lead a culminating discussion, focusing on cooperation and teamwork.

Discussion Questions:

1. What specific things did individual team members do that helped the team successfully guess words?
2. What specific behaviors made guessing difficult?
3. How well did your team work together?
4. Did any members of your team dominate the game? Why? What effect did this have?
5. Were any members of your team left out? Why? What effect did this have?
6. What could you do to improve your teamwork?

Variations:

With younger students, take a more active role by coaching the teams and writing the letters or portions of words on the board. Use age/grade-appropriate vocabulary words.

Outline for Friendship

A Counselor Activity

Overall Purpose:

This activity encourages students to be somewhat analytical about the important topic of friendship, describing how friends are made and what qualities are needed to keep them.

Materials:

One copy of the experience sheet, *What I Want in a Friend* for each student; a large sheet of butcher paper; marking pens; masking tape

Directions:

Announce to the students that today you have come to get some information from them about friendships. To develop interest, ask a few questions, such as:
- How many of you have friends?
- How many of you have a best friend?
- How do you know that this person is your friend?
- How many of you have a friend now that you didn't have a year ago?
- How did you and your friend meet?
- What did you and your friend say or do that caused a friendship to start?

Focus the discussion on how friendships develop. Encourage the students to identify such activities as walking to school together, being on a team or in a club together, taking music, dance, or karate lessons together, etc., and on such behaviors as offering to help someone solve a tough math problem, complimenting a person's appearance, starting conversations with kids you don't know, saying "hi" and "how are you?", and congratulating others when they score a point, do well on a test, or win a prize. Jot ideas on the board and verbally summarize the main points students come up with.

Distribute the student experience sheets and briefly review the directions. Give the students a few minutes to complete their sheets.

While the students are working, clear a space and lay the sheet of butcher paper on the floor. When the students have completed their experience sheets, ask four volunteers to join you in front of the group. Have one volunteer lie down on the butcher paper while two volunteers hold the paper down at either end to keep it from moving or curling. Ask the fourth volunteer to draw around the one who is lying down, using the marking pen.

Ask the volunteers to tape the drawing to a wall, and say: *We have here the outline of a best friend.*

Then, in your own words, explain:

I'm going to go around the room and have each of you describe one quality from your experience sheet that you think a best friend should have. When it's your turn, try to name a quality that hasn't been mentioned yet. I'm going to make all of these qualities part of my "best friend" here on the wall.

As the students describe qualities, write or symbolize them inside the outline. For example, if a student says, *I want my best friend to be kind*, draw a heart shape in the chest area and write the word *kind* inside it.

When everyone has had an opportunity to contribute, ask the questions below to facilitate a summary discussion.

Discussion Questions:

1. If you wanted to make a new friend, which of these qualities would be most helpful?
2. What kinds of things can you do to show a friend that you are thoughtful?
3. What kinds of things can you do to show that you are loyal?
4. What can you do to prove that you are truthful?
5. How can you demonstrate that you are interested in another person?
6. What is one area in which you could improve, in order to be a better friend?

Variations:

Have the students take turns adding qualities to the "perfect friend" outline themselves. After each person has written or symbolized a quality, ask him or her to explain to the group why that quality is important.

With young children, skip the experience sheet and generate ideas directly from the group. Symbolize or write the qualities within the outline as simply and clearly as possible. Read each word back to the students and ask them to read it with you.

What I Want in a Friend

Student Experience Sheet

What qualities do you value in a friend? Read through the list and circle the 10 qualities that are most important to you. Then write them on the poster that the student is holding. Rank the qualities from most important on the first line to the least important on the last line.

I want my best friend to be:

ambitious
artistic
athletic
beautiful
brave
considerate
clever
creative
dedicated
dependable
energetic
fair
gentle
generous
graceful
funny
fun to be with
handsome
happy
helpful
honest
humble
intelligent
kind
a good listener
loyal
neat
organized

patient
polite
popular
rich
sensitive
serious
smart

strong
talented
thoughtful
truthful
understanding
witty

I Want My Friend To Be...

1. _____
2. _____
3. _____
4. _____
5. _____
6. _____
7. _____
8. _____
9. _____
10. _____

A Commercial Friendship Break

A Counselor/Teacher Activity

Overall Purpose:

In this activity the students zero in on qualities and behaviors that define good friendships, and they do it in a focused and highly creative way — by making TV commercials selling a partner's friendship characteristics. In order to ensure that their TV commercials "sell," the students must become very committed to them, and to the classmates they represent.

Materials:

One copy of the experience sheet, *Do I Have a Friend for You!* for each student; any costume or prop items that can be made available in the classroom

Directions:

Tell the students that today they are going to find out what good friends exist right there in the classroom.

Distribute the experience sheets, and have the students pair up. (Random pairing works best for this activity.) Tell them to decide who is **A** and who is **B**.

In your own words, explain the activity:

*You are going to interview your partner to find out what a good friend he or she makes. Ask the questions on your experience sheet, and write down the answers that your partner gives you. **A** will be the first interviewer. After 4 minutes, I'll call time and tell you to switch roles. Then, **B** will be the interviewer for 4 minutes.*

Keep an eye on the clock, telling the students to switch roles after 4 minutes. When the interviews have been completed, explain the next part of the activity:

With your partner in the lead role, I want you to create a 1-minute commercial selling your partner's friendship qualifications to the rest of us. You are going to do your very best to convince us to "buy" your partner as a friend. There are many ways you can do this. You could have your partner act out certain characteristics or talents. You could parade your partner up and down while you talk about his or her good qualities. Or you could have your partner do the selling by singing a jingle or reciting a poem. Think about commercials you've seen on TV and remember how the products were pictured and described. If you like, do a "take off" on a specific TV commercial. Feel free to use any props that you can find around the classroom. You'll have just 30 minutes to plan and rehearse both commercials, so get started!

Both you and the teacher should circulate and help the students develop their commercials. Urge them to be creative — even outrageous. Make the activity lively and fun.

In a second session, have the students present their commercials. Applaud after each one. Then lead a culminating discussion focusing on the qualities most valued in friends.

Discussion Questions:

1. What friendship qualities did you see and hear most often in our commercials?
2. Do you think we have to "sell" ourselves to others? Explain.
3. Did you learn something about a classmate that you didn't know before? What was it?
4. What, for you, was the most interesting part of this activity?

Variations:

Share responsibility for this activity with the teacher. Facilitate the introduction and the commercial-planning process. Then, have the teacher lead the presentations, perhaps spreading them over several sessions. Try to get back to class to see as many commercials as possible.

For very young students, come up with two or three simple interview questions, write them on the board and go over them several times. Omit the experience sheet.

Do I Have a Friend for You!

Student Experience Sheet

Ask your partner the questions below. Write down his or her answers. Then use what you've learned to create a TV commercial. The purpose of the commercial is to "sell" your partner's friendship qualities to the rest of the class. Be convincing! Be daring! Have fun!

1. What are your favorite activities? _____
   _____
   _____
   _____

2. What sports or hobbies do you enjoy most? _____
   _____
   _____
   _____
   _____
   _____

3. What is your best school subject? _____
   _____

4. What do your friends like best about you? _____
   _____
   _____
   _____
   _____

5. What do you like best about yourself? _____
   _____
   _____
   _____
   _____

6. What have you made or done that you're proud of? _____
   _____
   _____
   _____
   _____

7. If you won the "Friend of the Year" award, what would the plaque say about you?
   _____
   _____
   _____
   _____

Responding Assertively to Peer Pressure

A Counselor/Teacher Activity

Overall Purpose:

To involve the students in defining peer pressure, generate relevant examples of peer pressure situations and styles, and apply and practice specific assertive behaviors geared to those situations and styles.

Materials:

One copy of the student experience sheet, *How to Handle Bullies, Chicken-Callers, and Other Peers Who Pressure You!* for each student (handed out by the teacher as reinforcement)

Directions:

Begin by asking the students if they have ever heard the term, *peer pressure*. Write the term on the board and ask the students to tell you what each word means. When you have established that one's peers are people the same age or grade, and that pressure is force or strong influence, ask the students to define the entire term. Write the definition on the board.

Next, ask the students: *In what kinds of situations might you feel pressured by your peers to do something that you don't feel okay doing?*

List on the board ideas that the students generate. They are likely to include:
- pressure to use alcohol and other drugs
- pressure to skip school
- pressure to do something or go somewhere that is "off limits"
- pressure to ignore, tease, or put down another student
- pressure to laugh at something that isn't really funny
- pressure to "go along" with the misbehavior of others
- pressure to cheat on tests or share homework

Point out that there are different styles of peer pressure. In your own words, explain:

Depending on the circumstances and who's doing the pressuring, peer pressure takes different forms. If we can recognize a style, we can respond in the most effective way.

Ask two students to help you role-play each of the following styles, using peer pressure situations from the list you have generated on the board. Set up each scenario and coach the actors through it. Allow the actors to continue their exchange for as long as it remains instructive. Try out different responses and ask the audience to rate their effectiveness. Dialogue suggestions are in italics below.

The Broken Record

This person repeats the same thing over and over, trying to wear down your resistance. Your challenge is to outlast the person, restating your refusal just as persistently.

Person A: *Oh, come on, one little drink won't hurt. Let's do it, come on!*
Person B: *No, I don't want to. I'm too young to drink alcohol.*
Person A: *Geez, just a little. Come on.*
Person B: *No, I'm not going to do it.*

The Yes, But-ter

This person likes to debate. He or she starts by challenging you with the question *Why not?* and, when you state your reason, tries to talk you out of it. Instead of endlessly arguing with such a person, suggest that he or she go ahead and do whatever it is alone.

Person A: *Why not?*
Person B: *Because I'm supposed to be in school.*
Person A: *Yes, but school is boring. The beach is fun.*
Person B: *I can go to the beach on Saturday. Today is a school day.*
Person A: *Yes, but Saturday the weather won't be so good.*
Person B: *Then I'll wait till it is good. If you think skipping school is such a good idea, go by yourself.*

The Chicken Caller

This person tries to trick you into proving that you're not afraid by calling you a chicken. Don't fall for it! There's nothing wrong with being reluctant to do something that's bad for you.

Person A: *Don't be a chicken. It's fun at Greg's house.*
Person B: *Greg's parents aren't home. I'm not supposed to be there.*
Person A: *Since when is the chicken so afraid of his parents?*
Person B: *Yes, I'm afraid. I don't want my parents mad at me, and I don't want to be restricted. I'm not going.*

The Bully

This person makes physical threats. He or she may threaten to start a fight or to hurt you in some way, and may hit or push to prove the point. Don't put up with physical abuse. Ask an adult to intervene. If no adult is nearby, leave the situation immediately.

Person A: *If you sit with Amy, you'll be sorry.*
Person B: *I like Amy. She's my friend and I like to sit with her.*
Person A: *If you don't want to get beat up, stay away from her (pushes B).*
Person B: *You can't push me around. I'm going to tell Ms. Macias.*

The Coercer

A person who tries to coerce you often uses bribes or threats related to your relationship or friendship. These people are usually bluffing. Since a real friend does not try to control you, stand up for yourself. Show that you have a mind of your own.

Person A: *If you don't let me copy your homework, you're not my friend.*
Person B: *I worked hard on my homework and I don't like giving it away.*
Person A: *You don't want me to get in trouble do you? If you were really my friend, you'd want to help me!*
Person B: *No. And this doesn't have anything to do with friendship.*

The Ridiculer

This person puts others down in an effort to get his or her way. Like the kid who yells, "chicken," the ridiculer hopes that you'll go along in order to prove that you're an okay person. Don't get hooked! You are okay, and you don't have to prove a thing.

Person A: *You're such a bore. Playing a trick on Robert will be fun.*
Person B: *It's not my idea of fun.*
Person A: *What a goody goody. You're just trying to act superior.*
Person B: *Yeah, maybe not wanting to hurt someone is superior. Count me out.*

The Reassurer

This person pretends to take all the responsibility, calming your fears and reassuring you that everything will be all right. Keep in mind that no one can guarantee a good outcome when what you are doing is wrong or dangerous. You have to look out for yourself.

Person A: *If we open the window the smoke will go outside.*
Person B: *My mom can smell smoke a block away. She'll know.*
Person A: *Don't worry. I do this at home all the time. Trust me.*
Person B: *No. If you want to smoke, you'll have to leave.*

Conclude the activity with a general discussion focusing on assertive behaviors. Ask the following questions or others that seem relevant based on the role plays. Leave the experience sheets with the teacher to pass out at the end of the day or the following day for reinforcement.

Discussion Questions:

1. Why do people try to pressure each other into doing things?
2. What kinds of things can you say to yourself when someone is pressuring you to do something that is wrong or dangerous?
3. If you have doubts about doing something, but aren't sure it's a bad idea, what can you say or do?
4. Why is it important to learn to stand up for yourself?
5. What are some other kinds of situations where you can practice being assertive?

Variations:

Make copies of the seven scenarios given here as examples. Distribute them to the students so that they can read their parts. Be sure to encourage variations and embellishments.

With primary-grade students, omit the labels and concentrate on teaching simple assertive behaviors. The familiar "Four Ways to Say No" works well.

1. Say no.
2. Say no and give a reason.
3. Say no and suggest something else to do.
4. Say no and leave.

How to Handle Bullies, Chicken-Callers, and Other Peers Who Pressure You!

Student Experience Sheet

Fill in the cartoon bubbles with the words you want each person to say. Make these kids stand up for themselves!

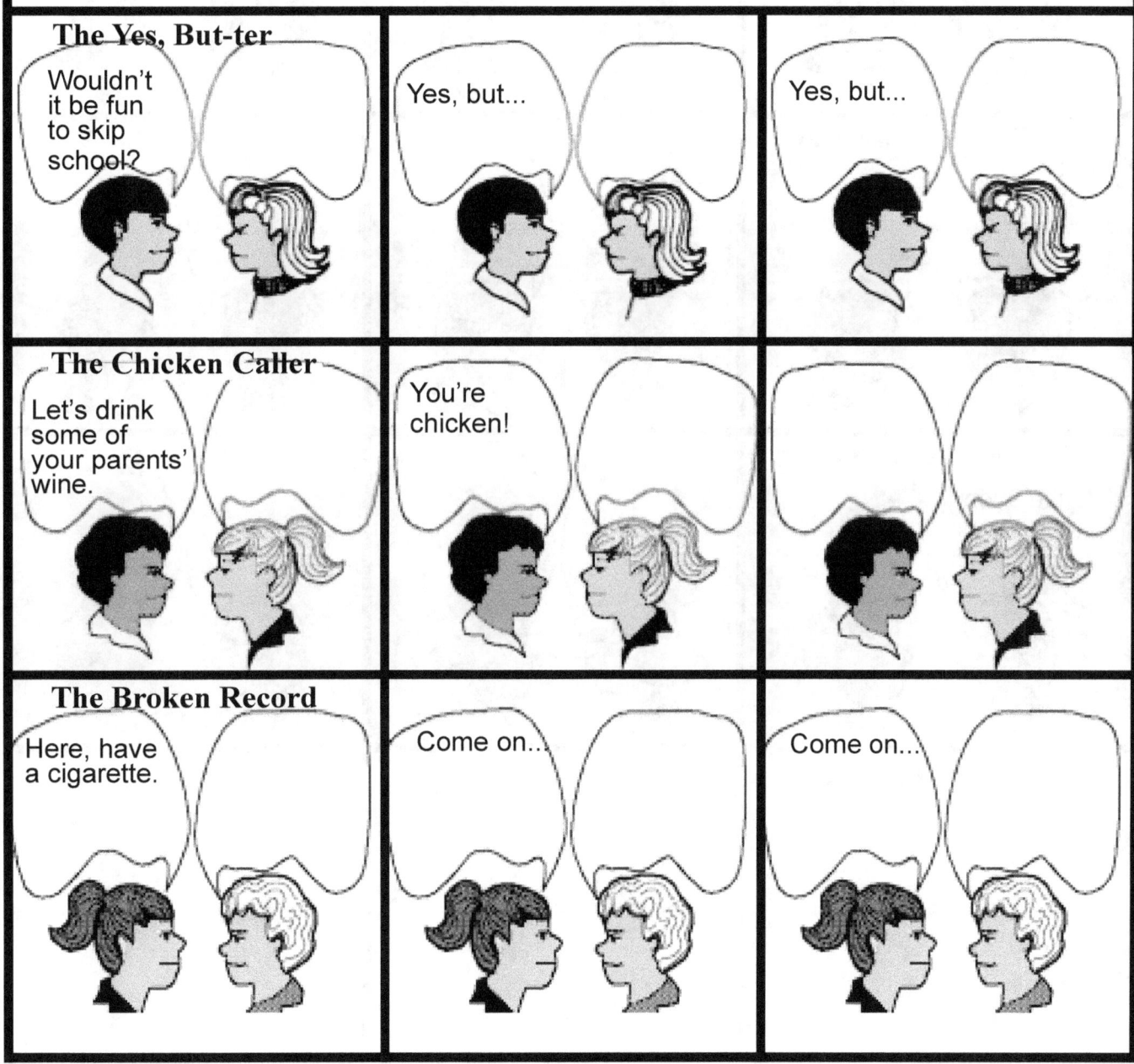

How To Handle Bully Behavior

A Counselor Activity

Overall Purpose:

This activity is designed to help students define, describe and understand bully behavior. It provides an opportunity for students to feel safe in sharing experiences they have had, and to learn that they are not alone in experiencing bully encounters. It also helps students understand how to report bullying incidences when they occur.

Procedure:

Ask the students to help you brainstorm a list of typical bully behaviors. Write them on the board. Add the following if they are not suggested by the group:

- demanding money or other objects
- hitting
- making fun of
- name-calling
- damaging personal belongings
- stealing
- laughing at
- yelling at
- excluding (leaving out of activities or groups)
- forcing to do something
- gossiping and telling lies about

Go back over each item on the list and ask for a show of hands from students who have experienced the bully behavior that you call out. Point out that all of these hurtful experiences are the result of bullying and should be stopped.

Directions:

Ask if anyone would like to talk to the group about his or her experience of having been bullied. Remind them to talk about what happened and how they felt, but not to use names. Break the ice by sharing a personal story of your own related to bullying.

Facilitate discussion following each sharing of personal bullying experiences. Stress that it is important for students to come forward if they are bullied, or witness someone else being bullied. Let the students know that bullying will not be tolerated; however, before bullying can be stopped, incidents of bullying must be reported and that you will be helping the students to develop strategies and actions for dealing with bullies.

Go on to point out that bullying incidents that happen at school often occur in busy places, like hallways, lunch areas, in front of the school and on playgrounds. Although adults don't ususally see these incidents, very often other kids are nearby and do witness these incidents, but don't know what to do.

Ask the students to help you brainstorm things that witnesses can do to stop bullies. Add the following four ideas if they are not mentioned by the group.

1. Refuse to watch a bullying incident. Bullies want an audience.
2. If appropriate and safe, distract the bully and/or victim.
3. Create safety in numbers. If you know that someone is being bullied, make sure that the victim is not alone in places where he or she is vulnerable.
4. Report bullying incidents.

Stress that reporting the incident is very important. Even if the students try other strategies to stop the bully, they should always tell a responsible adult what happened.

Write the following headings on the board:

Who   How

Stress that students should talk to an adult about every bullying incident that occurs. Under Who, list appropriate adults.

Next, discuss ways of reporting that guard the safety of students, such as writing an anonymous note, going to the office after school when the rest of the kids have gone home, or calling a teacher or counselor from home. List these ideas under How.

Stress that anyone can feel safe in coming to you or the teacher for help with bullying. Make a distinction between tattling or snitching and reporting an incident. Tattling is about wanting to get someone in trouble. Informing an adult is about wanting to help a victim.

As a class follow-up, ask the teacher to have the students create a poster of the Who and How list and display it in the class so that it can serve as a reminder and reinforcement of what the students can do about bullying.

Conclude the activity by discussing when and how to ask for help. Use the discussion questions below, and other appropriate questions. Encourage the students to practice the actual words they would say when asking for help.

Discussion Questions:

1. How do you feel when you see someone acting like a bully? What do you usually do?
2. Why is it important to let bullies know that their behavior is unacceptable?
3. If you were on your way to school and a bully forced you to hand over your skate board, or jacket, or lunch, to whom would you go for help? When should you go?
4. If a group of kids were making your life miserable with insults, taunts, and teasing, and you decided to ask me for help, how would you explain the situation to me?
5. If you saw a bully beating up on another student, when and how would you take action? What would you say?

Sending I Messages
A Counselor Activity

Overall Purpose:

This activity gives students an opportunity to learn and practice I messages, a skill for effectively expressing their thoughts, feelings, and wants.

Materials:

One copy of the experience sheet, *Getting Your Message Across*, for each student

Directions:

Talk to the students about the importance of sending clear, sincere messages to other people. If you have already completed a listening activity with the students, point out that speaking is the other half of the communication process. Emphasize that sending clear messages is particularly important when talking to people who are not good listeners, which unfortunately includes all people some of the time, and many people all of the time. Being heard and understood takes care and effort.

Distribute the experience sheets and go over the first part with the students. Clarify the 6-step process listed on the first page of experience sheet. Ask the students why each step is important and give examples.

1. Ask to be heard.
2. Look directly at the listener.
3. Speak in a clear voice.
4. Use "I" Messages
5. Check for understanding.
6. Thank the listener

Next, focus on the process for formulating an "I" message. Write the steps as headings across the top of the board. They are: Describe the situation; state how you feel the situation is affecting you: and, say what you want. Underneath the headings begin to construct examples. (Use the examples provided or think of others that are more relevant.)

- Describe the situation — the person's behavior or the conditions that are causing you a problem.

"When you...
 ...interrupt me so much...
 ...borrow my sweater without asking...
 ...keep the kitten in your room all the time...
 ...say things behind my back...
 ...question me so much...

- State how you feel and how the situation is affecting you.

"I feel...
 ...frustrated because I can't finish a sentence...
 ...irritated because the sweater isn't here when I want it...
 ...sad because I never get to play with her...
 ...hurt, because you're my friend...
 ...like you don't trust me.

- Say what you want.

"I'd like you to...
 ...listen to me tell my story."
 ...ask me before you take something."
 ...share her with me."
 ...stop talking about me when I'm not around."
 ...believe me when I tell you something."

Have the students complete the second part of their experience sheet, constructing practice "I" messages. Invite several students to read their "I" messages to the class. Then involve the students in thinking of other typical situations. Together, develop an "I" message for each one.

Conclude the activity with a summary discussion.

Discussion Questions:

1. What is the most difficult part about sending "I" messages?
2. What are some other ways in which people communicate what they want?
3. Why is sending an "I" message more effective than demanding what you want?
4. How do you feel when someone blames or criticizes you?
5. Are you more apt to listen to an "I" message or a blaming, criticizing message? Why?
6. How are you going to use this skill? When are you going to start?

Variations:

Role play some of the situations. Have the actors try less effective ways of communicating their wishes, like demanding, whining, criticizing, name calling, etc., and then substitute an "I" message. Discuss the differences in effectiveness (getting the job done) and the impact on the listener and the relationship (feelings).

Getting Your Message Across
Student Experience Sheet

When you want to be heard, send a clear message. Follow these steps:

1. Ask to be heard.
    - "I'd like to talk to you."
    - "There's something I want to say."

2. Look directly at the listener

3. Speak in a clear voice.

4. Use "I" Messages

    - Describe the situation
        "When you..."

    - State how you feel.
        "I feel..."

    - Say what you want.
        "I'd like you to..."

5. Check for understanding.

6. Thank the listener

Practice writing some "I" messages here:

• You are having a conversation with a friend, but your friend keeps interrupting you. You are getting upset, so you decide to use an "I" message.

When you _____

_____

I feel _____

and I'd like you to _____

_____

_____

• You are trying to study at home. The TV is so loud in the next room that you can't think. You decide to explain how the noise is affecting you.

When you _____

_____

I feel _____

_____

and I'd like you to _____

_____

_____

Developing Listening Skills
A Counselor Activity

Overall Purpose:

Use this activity to introduce important communication concepts, and to give students an opportunity to learn and practice skills associated with active listening.

Materials:

One copy of the experience sheet, *Active Listening*, for each student; several topics written on the board prior to the session (see suggestions below)

Directions:

Tell the students that today they will be practicing one of the most important communication skills they will ever learn — Active Listening. Write the term on the board, underline the word Active, and ask the students how they think active listening differs from the kind of listening they do all day long, every day.

Accept all ideas and begin to facilitate a discussion about the importance of listening. You might ask the students how they feel when someone really listens to them, and what it feels like to be interrupted or to realize that the other person didn't hear a word they said. In the course of your discussion, make the following points about listening:
- Good listeners are rare.
- In most conversations, people are more concerned with what they want to say than what the other person is saying.
- Good listening requires focus, concentration, and energy.
- To really listen, you have to keep an open mind and heart.
- Listening all by itself is the most effective way to help another person solve a problem or make a decision.

Distribute the experience sheets. Go over the steps to active listening.

Four Steps to Active Listening

1. Look at the person who is talking.
2. Listen carefully to his or her words.
3. Notice the feelings that go with the words.
4. Say something to show that you have been listening.

Discuss specific behaviors involved in each step. For example, point out that listening to the words requires thinking about and understanding their meaning *from the speaker's point of view*. Noticing feelings involves paying attention to the speaker's tone of voice, facial expression, and posture, and *empathizing* — imagining what it would be like to be in the speaker's shoes. Saying something back not only proves that you are listening, it helps the speaker clarify his or her thoughts and allows you to check to make sure you are "getting the message."

Demonstrate with a volunteer. Ask a student to join you in the front of the room and to talk for a couple of minutes about something that is important to him or her. Instruct the class to watch carefully and notice what you do. Allow the demonstration to continue long enough for you to give four or five active listening responses. Then thank the volunteer and ask the observers to describe what they saw. Clarify the process and answer questions.

Have the students form teams of two and decide who will be **A** and who will be **B**. Ask each team to choose a topic from the board. In your own words, give the teams these instructions:

Each of you will speak to the topic you have chosen for 2 minutes while your partner is listening. ***A*** *will speak first for 2 minutes while* ***B*** *listens and demonstrates active listening. Then* ***B*** *will take 30 seconds to tell* ***A*** *what he or she said. Then you will switch roles.* ***B*** *will talk and* ***A*** *will listen. I will call time each time you switch.*

Time the 2-minutes of **A** talking and the activie listening response by **B**. Signal when it is time to switch. (The clear but unobtrusive tone of a chime or bell works well for this purpose.) After every student has had a turn to speak and to listen, briefly ask each group how it went, clarifying further, as needed. Then, if time allows, have the groups choose a second topic and repeat the procedure.

Conclude the activity with a summary discussion.

Discussion Questions:

1. What was the easiest thing about active listening.
2. What was most difficult?
3. How did it feel to be listened to?
4. Why do people so seldom stop and really listen to each other?
5. How do you think active listening helps people solve problems?
6. How does this process relate to listening at school, for example, listening to the teacher and understanding assignments?
7. What do you need to work on in order to become a better listener?

Variations:

For more concentrated group practice (with older students), have one student at a time discuss a concern, while the other members of the group take turns giving active-listening responses to the student who is speaking. To equalize practice, the responders should be instructed to take their turn in order, going around the circle clockwise. Remind the speakers to pause after every few sentences so that the next listener can respond. Give each speaker about 5 minutes to talk. Then signal the groups to change speakers.

Discussion Topics:

What I'd like to do this weekend
A skill I'm trying to improve
Something I'm worried about
My hardest subject in school
The best time I ever had with a friend
The best vacation I ever had
Something I'm looking forward to

Active Listening
Student Experience Sheet

What is Active Listening? It's when you listen very carefully and try to understand the ideas and feelings of another person *from his or her point of view.*

Four Steps to Active Listening

1. Look at the person who is talking.
2. Listen carefully to his or her words.
3. Notice the feelings that go with the words.
4. Say something to show that you have been listening.

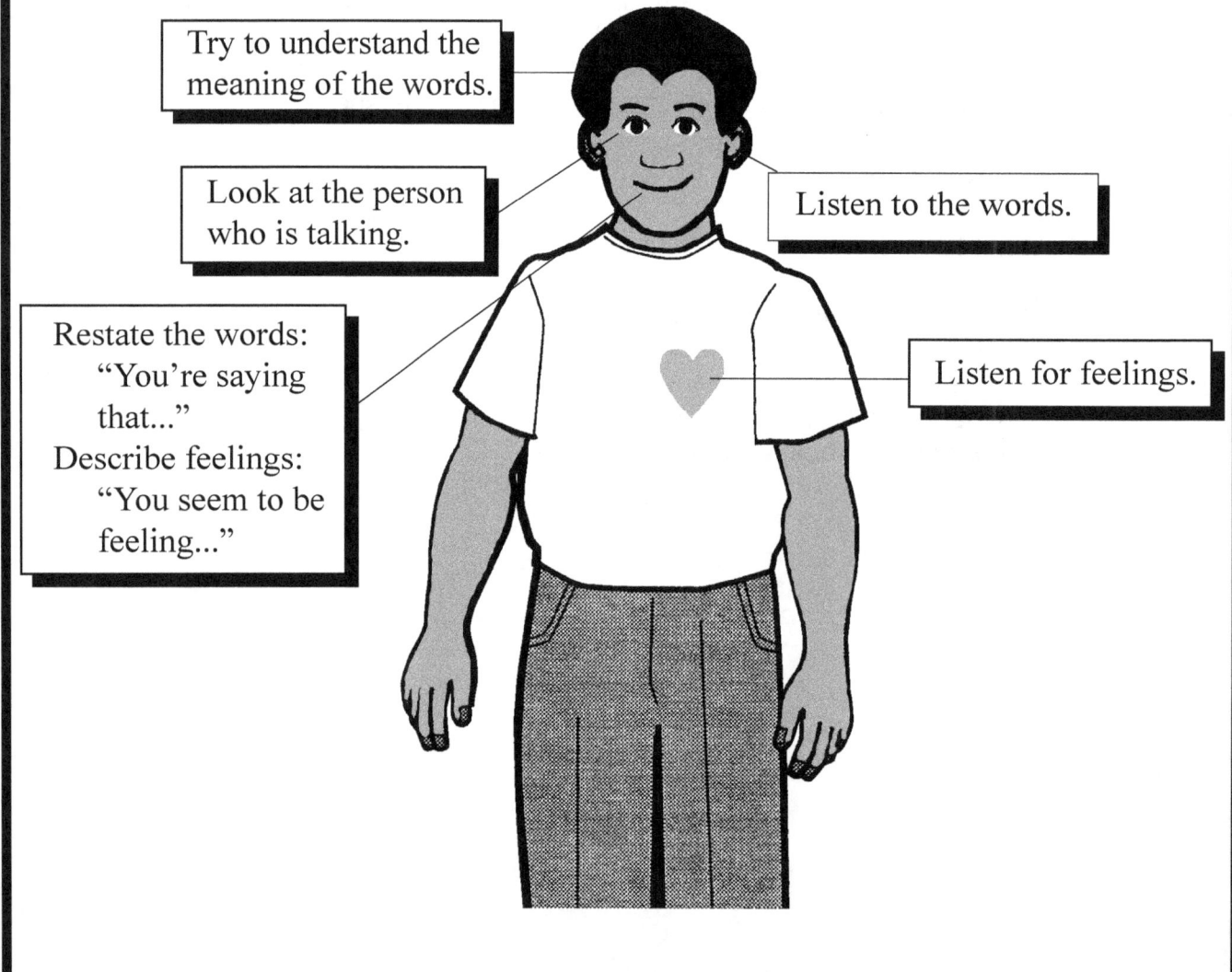

Try to understand the meaning of the words.

Look at the person who is talking.

Listen to the words.

Restate the words: "You're saying that..."
Describe feelings: "You seem to be feeling..."

Listen for feelings.

Listening to Directions
A Counselor Activity

Overall Purpose:

This activity deals specifically with effective listening in situations (common to children) involving one-way communication. After reviewing strategies for effective listening, the students have an opportunity to test their ability to hear and follow directions accurately.

Materials:

Paper and pencils

Directions:

Begin by asking the students: *How do you know when someone is listening to you?*

Accept all responses, jotting ideas on the board. For example, the listener usually:
— looks at me
— is quiet
— shows understanding
— asks questions that make sense
— doesn't interrupt

Point out that, while conversations are an example of two-way communication, there are also many times when communication is mostly one-way. Some of them are very important. Ask the students to help you think of examples of one-way communication in which good listening is very important. Generate a list that includes such instances as:
— when you are lost and ask for directions
— when your teacher gives an assignment
— when your parents tell you where and when to meet them
— when someone is teaching you a new skill
— when the operator is giving you a phone number
— when the principal is explaining a change in schedule over the intercom

Announce that the students are going to see how good they are at listening to one-way communication. Tell them to start right now by listening carefully to your instructions.

Distribute paper and pencils. Tell the students that they have 1 minute to draw a simple design using a circle, a triangle, a rectangle, one curved line, and two straight lines. Write a list of the elements on the board. Tell them to arrange the elements any way they wish in any size they wish.

When the students have finished, tell them to fold their drawings to hide them from view, and form a dyad with one other person. In your own words, explain the task:

*First decide who is **A** and who is **B**. Then turn your desks or chairs and sit back to back. When it is your turn to be the speaker, you will open your drawing and slowly and clearly describe it to your partner. Your partner will attempt to duplicate the drawing on the back of his or her own sheet. When you are the listener, do not speak or turn around, just listen and draw. You will have 2 minutes to complete the drawing. When I call time, switch roles. Repeat the process for another 2 minutes. The **A's** will be the first speakers.*

Clarify and answer questions. Then start the exercise, keeping time and signaling the students to switch roles after 2 minutes. When both rounds are completed, tell the partners to turn around and compare their drawings. Urge them to comment on each other's effectiveness as a speaker and listener.

Lead a follow-up discussion

Discussion Questions:

1. What was the hardest part about this exercise? What was the easiest part?
2. What was it like when you were the speaker?
3. What role does listening play in following directions?
4. What kinds of things can happen as a result of poor listening?
5. What kinds of things make it hard to understand directions and other kinds of one-way communication?
6. What should you do if you don't understand?

Variations:

Use the same activity to focus on speaking skills — or both speaking and listening skills. Brainstorm and discuss the process of sending messages clearly and accurately.

Asking for Help
A Counselor Activity

Overall Purpose:

This activity helps the students understand some of the dynamics of needing, asking for, and receiving help. In addition, the students identify, contrast, and discuss effective and ineffective ways of seeking help.

Materials:

One copy of the experience sheet, *The Help Line*, for each student

Directions:

Get the students' attention by writing the exclamation *HELP!* in large letters on the board. Wait a few moments to pique their curiosity and then ask them: *What is help?*

Listen to their ideas and when everyone seems to agree on a definition, say: *Describe examples of times when you or I might need help.*

Make a list of suggestions on the board, including such situations as:
- When you feel sick
- When you injure yourself.
- When you don't understand an assignment.
- When you can't solve a math problem
- When someone threatens to hurt you.
- When someone tries to give or sell you drugs.
- When you witness an accident, crime, or fight.
- When you can't study at home.
- When you're not getting your schoolwork done and you don't know why.
- When you keep getting low grades no matter how hard you try.
- When you feel so worried or depressed about something that you can't concentrate.

As you record the students' suggestions, feed back your understanding of the feelings they might have under those circumstances, e.g., *Yes, Mat, and you'd probably be feeling pretty scared if that happened.* or *No matter how hard you try, Sue, when you feel worried it's awfully hard to think about social studies or spelling words.*

Draw a line down the middle of the board and write the headings "Effective" and "Ineffective" on either side of the line at the top. Next, select one situation and develop a brief scenario around it so that the students can imagine themselves in the situation. For example, say: *You're sitting there and all the other kids have started working. You see them getting out paper and books, some are starting to move around the room, and some are writing. It hits you that you have absolutely no idea what you are supposed to be doing. What are some ineffective ways of asking for help in this situation? What are some effective ways?*

Record suggestions under the appropriate heading, discussing each one briefly. For example, yelling across the room to a friend would be ineffective because it would irritate the teacher and disrupt the class. Going up to the teacher and explaining your confusion (without interrupting) would probably be effective.

Follow the same procedure with other situations from the list. Use your knowledge as a counselor to give the students some insights into destructive, compensating, and withdrawing behaviors that are ineffective cries for help. Use examples that illustrate how common such reactions are among children and adults alike. Take your time with this part of the activity, giving examples that the students can relate to.

Distribute the experience sheet, *The Help Line*. Clarify the directions and give the students a couple of minutes to complete the task. Then ask the students to form groups of six to eight. Direct them to take turns sharing their experience sheet and explaining why they decided to place themselves in a particular position on the "help line."

Allow 5 to 10 minutes for sharing. Then reconvene the class and facilitate a culminating discussion.

Discussion Questions:

1. How do you feel when you get help that you need?
2. How do you feel when someone insists on helping you, even though you don't want help?
3. What are some reasons that you might hesitate to ask for help?
4. In what kinds of situations should you always ask for help?
5. What can you do if you need help and no one is around to ask?

Variations:

Divide the class into teams and role play several of the scenarios from the brainstormed list of situations in which help is needed. Have each group of actors go through their scenario twice — dramatizing first an ineffective way of asking for help, and then an effective way.

With younger students, draw the Help Line on the board (instead of using the experience sheet). Illustrate Helpless Harry at one end and describe him. Draw a picture of Island Iris at the other end and describe her. Exaggerate the differences to make the characters funny. Then ask the students to come up and write their names somewhere on the line to show what kind of "help-seekers" they are.

The Help Line!
Student Experience Sheet

How much of a help-seeker are you? The line below is called a continuum. It's a help-seeking continuum. Harry is at one end of the continuum — asking for help all the time. Iris is at the other end of the continuum — refusing help all the time. Write your name or draw a picture of yourself somewhere on the line. Choose the spot that best shows how much of a help-seeker you are!

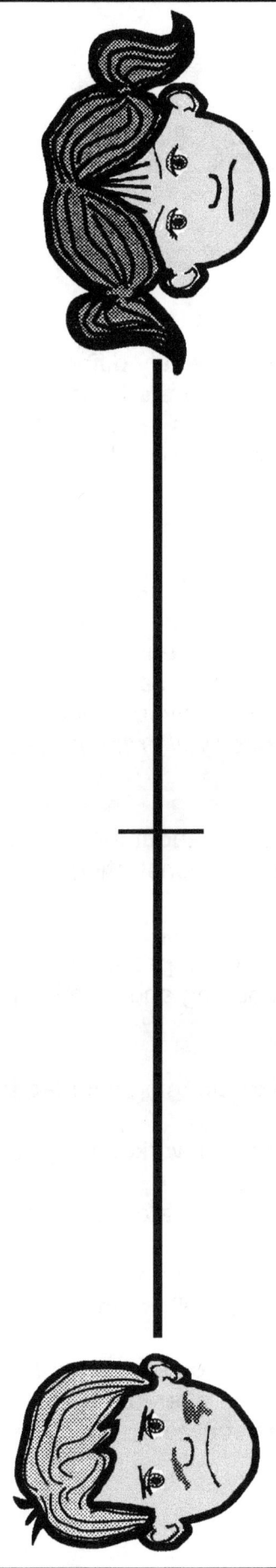

Helpless, Hapless Harry

Harry can't do anything by himself. If you tell him to turn to page 54 in his book, he whines that he can't find it. If he gets a tiny cut on his finger, you think his whole arm is about to fall off. When the teacher asks if anyone has a question, Harry's hand is always the first in the air. When it's Harry's turn to carry equipment in from the field, he complains and stumbles and drags his feet. It's easy to imagine Harry being carried around and waited on by a company of servers. Harry demands help all the time.

I-Am-an-Island Iris

Iris pretends she can handle anything by herself. If she doesn't understand an assignment, she pretends. She can spend hours figuring out what to do when one question would settle the matter in less than a minute. If she hurts herself, "it's nothing," even when the blood is streaming down her face. Iris won't tell anyone when she's worried or scared. You can actually see her get smaller as she burrows into herself. Her hair may be standing on end, but her mouth is set and stern, and her voice is firm: "No thank you. I don't need any help."

Control Yourself!
A Counselor Activity

Overall Purpose:

This activity allows students to identify different kinds of self-control and self-management, to demonstrate behaviors associated with self-control in a variety of situations, and to publicly affirm how they feel about their own levels of self-control.

Directions:

Begin this session by asking the students what the term self-control means. Listen to and reflect the students' responses. In the process, establish that having self-control means being able to restrain and regulate one's own behavior. Then say: *Think of a time when your emotions were so strong that you couldn't control yourself. Maybe you didn't want to cry or yell or laugh, but the feelings were overpowering.*

Invite volunteers to tell the class about their experiences. Ask one or two to act out their incidents, demonstrating exactly what happened.

Next, whisper one of the following situations to a volunteer and have that student act out the situation in pantomime (nonverbally). Have the class guess what is happening and identify the emotion that the student is trying to control.

— You just crashed your bike, banging your leg badly, in front of several older kids.
— You get back a paper that you worked very hard on. It's covered with red marks and graded C-.
— Walking home at dusk, you turn a corner and practically run right into a big skunk.
— While your teacher is explaining an assignment, you see another student do something hysterically funny and try to keep from breaking up.
— Your parent restricts you for something your brother or sister did.
— You are walking home alone after just learning that a boy or girl you have a crush on likes you, too.

Repeat this process with the remainder of the situations and a new volunteer each time. After each pantomime, talk about methods typically used to control reactions to various emotions (biting tongue, clenching fists, taking deep breaths, blinking, stiffening muscles, looking away, etc.)

Draw a long horizontal line across the board. At one end write "Volcanic Vicki." At the other end write, "Restrained Robert." Explain to the students that the line is a *self-control continuum* and that Vicki and Robert represent the extreme endpoints. Ask the students to help you describe Vicki and Robert. Have fun with this and encourage the students to exaggerate their descriptions. For example:

Volcanic Vicki is going off all the time. At the slightest provocation, steam spews from her nostrils, tears from her eyes, and agonizing, earth shaking sounds from her throat. Vicki was once able to control herself for 20 seconds, and that was when a bee landed on her nose.

Restrained Robert looks a little like an automated store mannequin. His expression almost never changes and his movements are stiff and controlled. People have exhausted themselves trying to make Robert laugh, or blink, or get angry. But Robert would rather die than lose control.

Ask two or three students at a time to write their names somewhere on the continuum. Explain that before they do this, they must decide how much self-control they have. Are they closer to Vicki's end of the continuum or Robert's? Give all of the students an opportunity to place themselves on the line.

Lead a culminating class discussion, focusing on the concepts of self-control and self-management. Then, with the last few minutes remaining, play a little game with the students. Tell them to sit absolutely still, without fidgeting, talking, or blinking. Explain that the last student to move is the winner. Time the students and proclaim the winner, "Self-control King" or "Self-control Queen" for the day.

Discussion Questions:

1. Why is it important to learn self-control?
2. What would school be like if students and teachers never made any effort to manage their feelings or behavior?
3. What does self-management have to do with responsibility?
4. What do your parents mean when they tell you to "be on your best behavior?"
5. How do you feel when you successfully control yourself?

Variations:

With younger students, draw an imaginary self-control line on the floor and have the children stand in the spot that represents their place on the continuum. Have two students act out the parts of Volcanic Vicki and Restrained Robert while standing at either end of the imaginary line.

Being Comfortable in School

A Counselor Activity

Overall Purpose:

This activity helps students recognize that the more they know about their school and how it works, the more comfortable they will feel in school. By identifying various school resources and how to use them, feelings of inclusion and interdependence are maximized.

Materials:

A rough drawing of the school complex to duplicate on the board or chart paper

Directions:

Begin by introducing the concept of the school as a community. In your own words, say to the students:

Every community has resources. Offices and businesses help people who live in the community obtain the things they need, get help, etc. A school works like that, too. Resources in the school exist to help students feel comfortable and capable as important members of the school community.

Ask the students to help you brainstorm a list of resources within the school. Include on the list:

People

- Teachers
- Principal
- School nurse
- Cafeteria workers
- Bus driver
- Custodian
- Librarian
- Classroom aides
- Playground aides
- Secretaries
- Parent volunteers
- Counselor and/or psychologist

Places and Things

- Library
- Cafeteria
- Playing field
- Public telephone
- Patio
- Handbooks
- Media center
- Computer center

Go back through the list and ask volunteers to answer questions about some of the resources. For example ask:
— *What services does the librarian provide?*
— *When might you need to use a classroom aide as a resource?*
— *What's the best way to use the resources of the learning center?*
— *Can you describe a time when you used one of these resources?*

Next, create a simple map of the school on the board or chart paper. Draw just the outlines and ask volunteers to come forward and label the various buildings and rooms. Involve the students in a discussion concerning the school layout. Ask:
— *Why is the principal's office in the front of the complex instead of the rear?*
— *Why is the cafeteria located over here?*
— *How do the busses pull up after school and why?*
— *Can you think of a better location for the library? Where and why?*

Conclude the activity by facilitating discussion focusing on the concept of the school-community.

Discussion Questions:

1. What are some reasons why a student might feel uncomfortable in school?
2. How does knowing about resources help you feel more comfortable in school?
3. If you need assistance in some way, but don't know where to find the correct resource, what can you do?
4. What have you learned from this activity?

Variations:

As a teacher follow-up to this activity, have the students work in teams of three or four to develop sections for a student handbook aimed at helping students understand the resources of the school and feel more comfortable in school. Begin by brainstorming an outline with the entire class. After the class has agreed on sections and general content, divide up the responsibilities. If computers are available, have the students use word processing and page layout programs to produce the final version of the handbook. Ask other students to illustrate the handbook, either by hand or with computer-generated art.

Developing Classroom Rules

A Counselor/Teacher Activity

Overall Purpose:

This activity involves students in developing their own set of classroom rules. In the process, the students are helped to understand the purpose of having rules and to experience a democratic group process for establishing rules.

Materials:

Large sheets of art paper, colored markers, and a prepared bulletin board on which to display the finished classroom rules.

Directions:

Talk to the teacher in advance about the kinds of rules needed in the classroom. It is important to achieve clarity concerning the needs of the teacher so that you can guide the students in appropriate directions during the activity. In addition, involve the teacher in discussions and in the final selection of rules.

Begin the activity by discussing with the students the need for rules in games and in group situations where people work together on a regular basis. Ask them: *What is the purpose of having rules in a game?*

Write suggestions on the board. For example, game rules:
- keep players safe.
- ensure that play is fair.
- give everyone an equal chance to participate.
- promote the purpose of the game.

Then ask: *Why do we have rules in the classroom?*

Again, record the responses of the students. For example, classroom rules:
- keep students safe.
- promote learning.
- give everyone an equal chance to participate.
- ensure the best use of time.
- encourage everyone to cooperate.

When the students appear to have a good understanding of the need and purpose for rules, divide them into small groups of four or five. Tell the groups that they have 10 minutes to brainstorm a list of rules that they think will help the classroom run smoothly and achieve the purposes listed on the board.

Ask each group to read its list of rules to the class. Write the suggested rules on the board. After all of the groups have reported, go back over the list to eliminate duplications. Then discuss and vote on each rule, inviting input from the teacher as well as students. Suggestions that receive a majority of votes become classroom rules.

Go back over the final list of rules and ask the students to help you identify rules that are worded negatively and rewrite them so that they are positive. For example, if a rule says, "No cutting in lines," it could be rewritten to say, "We always take our proper turn in line."

Have the students return to their small groups. Distribute the art paper and marking pens, and then divide the rules evenly among the small groups (indicating assignments on the board adjacent to the rules). In your own words, explain the next step:

Print one rule on each sheet of paper. Make the letters large enough to be seen from a distance. Then, draw a picture to illustrate the rule. Decide as a group how you want to divide up these responsibilities. You'll have 15 minutes to complete your rule sheets.

Ask each group to show its rules to the class before posting them on a bulletin board. Complete the activity with a brief discussion.

Discussion Questions:

1. How do you think this list of rules will help you personally?
2. What do you think the consequences should be for breaking a rule?
3. How does it feel to have a part in making the rules you live by?
4. If you act against a rule, whose rule are you actually breaking?
5. How is this process the same as or different from what happens when elected representatives make the rules that govern our city, state, and nation?

Variations:

Suggest that the teacher take this activity a step further by allowing a group of students to bind the rules into book form. The rule book could then be available throughout the year for review by students who break rules, and for revisions if rules need to be changed, added, or deleted.

You and the teacher may wish to alternate responsibility for various parts of this activity, spreading it over two or three days. For example, you could facilitate the initial brainstorming, the teacher could lead the development of classroom rules, and you could return to view the rules and facilitate a final discussion.

A Safety Quiz
A Counselor Activity

Overall Purpose:

This activity gives students an opportunity to test what they already know about making safety-conscious choices. Situations presented in the quiz then offer the basis for making a number of important points about responsible, safe behaviors.

Materials:

One copy of the experience sheet, *What Would You Do?* for each student

Directions:

Tell the students that the subject of this visit is safety. Explain that they are going to have an opportunity to see how much they already know about being safe at home, at school, and in their neighborhoods, and when going to and from various places.

Distribute the experience sheet, *What Would You Do?* and go over the directions with the students. Assure the students that they will not be graded on the quiz — that it is intended to give them information about how their decisions and actions affect their safety. Urge the students to think carefully about what they would do in each situation described.

Allow the students plenty of time to complete the quiz. When they have finished, go over the answers one at a time, discussing each situation. Welcome any ideas that the students present and encourage them to consider various alternatives and consequences. Stress that these are the best answers, given the amount of information conveyed, but that other actions might be even better depending on what else is actually going on in the situation.

ANSWERS:

1. (B)	9. (A)
2. (N)	10. (M)
3. (F)	11. (L)
4. (G)	12. (C)
5. (O)	13. (I)
6. (J)	14. (D)
7. (K)	15. (H)
8. (E)	

Conclude the activity by facilitating a summary discussion.

Discussion Questions:

1. What information should you give your parents before you go anywhere?
2. What is the "buddy system" and how does it help keep you safe?
3. What are some situations in which you should firmly say no?
4. What are some situations in which your first action should be to leave?
5. What kinds of situations should you report to a parent, teacher or other trusted adult?
6. How does talking about safety like this help you?
7. Who deserves to be safe?

Variations:

With lower-grade students, don't necessarily omit the experience sheet. Consider sending it home to parents. In class, describe each situation and two or three alternative actions. Ask the children, "Which is best?" Then discuss the reasons why certain behaviors create more safety than others.

Ask groups of students to role play situations from the experience sheet. The dramatizations can be as elaborate or as simple as you and the class want to make them. Coach the actors through each performance, inviting the audience to suggest alternative actions and trying them out as well. Focus on the possible consequences of each action.

What Would You Do? A Safety Quiz

Student Experience Sheet

You make decisions every day. Some decisions involve your safety. The numbered items below describe situations that you might face. The lettered items describe actions you could take to deal with those situations. Read each situation and pick the best action. Write the letter of that action on the line.

___ 1. You are on your way to a friend's house and you think a car is following you.

___ 2. You ride your bike to the store.

___ 3. You see a friend hitching a ride.

___ 4. You received money for your birthday and want to spend it at the mall.

___ 5. You are at the music store, and your friend wants to shoplift a CD.

___ 6. You must take your house key to school.

___ 7. A stranger tells you that he or she has been sent to take you home from school.

___ 8. You are playing in your yard when a neighbor asks, "Can you help me with these groceries?"

___ 9. You just got a really cool new backpack for your birthday.

___ 10. You're walking down the street. A car pulls up beside you and the driver says, "My dog is lost. If you'll help me find her, I'll pay you."

___ 11. A stranger bothers you in a movie.

___ 12. You have just witnessed a robbery.

___ 13. You are home alone and the doorbell rings. A voice from outside says, "Is anyone home? I need to check your phone."

___ 14. You need to call for help on a cell phone.

___ 15. Your bike has been stolen.

A. Mark it with your name and address before you take it to school.

B. If it is nearby, go immediately to your friend's house; if not, run in the opposite direction. Tell an adult what happened.

C. Remember what you saw and report it to the police.

D. Dial 911.

E. Say that you have to ask your parent first. Don't go inside anyone's home with your parent's approval.

F. Tell him or her that it's a bad idea and dangerous.

G. Go shopping with a friend or parent. If a friend, ask your parent to drop you off and pick you up.

H. You are the victim and should call the police.

I. Keep the door closed and locked. Call a neighbor and describe what happened.

J. Carry it inside your clothing.

K. Call your parent(s) to make sure.

L. Move and tell an usher.

M. Stay away from the car. Go tell an adult what happened.

N. Lock it well.

O. Try to talk your friend out of it. If you can't, don't go along.

Identities and Actions: A Lesson in Safety

A Counselor Activity

Overall Purpose:

This activity ensures that students know and can tell their names, addresses, and telephone numbers, and gives them specific things to do in threatening or dangerous situations. This is especially important for young children.

Materials:

A class roster with full names, addresses, and phone numbers of students (obtained from the office or teacher); chart paper and markers

Directions:

Begin by asking the students: *What is one of the most important things that your parents gave you when you were born?*

When the students guess "my name," point out that each student is a special person and therefore has a special name that tells other people who they are.

Ask the students to sit in a large circle, and announce that you are going to play an identification game. Explain that in this game you will be going around the circle several times and asking the students to say a little more about themselves each time.

Try to complete four rounds. Start off each round by modeling the information you want to hear from the students. Refer to the class list, as necessary, to coach younger students.

First round:
> first, middle, and last name (*My name is Cynthia Lynn Evans.*)

Second round:
> name and age (*My name is Cynthia Lynn Evans and I am 6 years old.*)

Third round:
> name, age, and address (*My name is Cynthia Lynn Evans, I am 6 years old, and I live at 3946 Water Street.*)

Fourth round:
> name, age, address, and phone number (*My name is Cynthia Lynn Evans, I am 6 years old, I live at 3946 Water Street, and my phone number is 299-2700.*)

At the conclusion of the game, congratulate the students for being able to recite so much about themselves.

Next, write these three words on the board: **NO — GO — TELL**. Ask the students what each word means. Facilitate discussion concerning the importance of remembering these words and what each stands for. Ask questions such as:

— When should you say no to another person?
— When should you shout no?
— When should you leave a place and go somewhere else?
— Where are some safe places to go?
— Where would you go if something happened on your way home from school?
— Where would you go if something happened riding your bike?
— What is a secret?
— What kinds of secrets are okay? ...not okay?
— To whom could you go if you needed help?
— Why is it important to tell a trusted adult if you feel scared or uncomfortable about something that has happened?

As the students respond to each question, make lists on the board under headings like, "When to Say NO," "When to GO," "Safe Places to GO," "When to TELL," and "People to TELL." Ask the teacher to display the lists on the bulletin board.

Discussion Questions:

1. Why is it important to trust your feelings and to tell someone when you feel afraid, confused, or uncomfortable?
2. Who is the number one person responsible for your safety?
3. What can you do to become a more safety-conscious person?

Variations:

Following the identification game, have/help the students print their name, address, and phone number on two 3" by 5" cards, one for their backpack, and one for their pocket. If possible, laminate the cards.

With older students, you may wish to omit the identification game or modify it by reducing the number of rounds or having students talk about where their parents work, how to contact police, fire department, etc.. One possibility is to challenge the students to create a short "Rap" containing their name, address, and phone number, and to complete one "Rap Round."

Safety Mapping

A Teacher Activity

Overall Purpose:

This is an activity that you can recommend to the teacher as a way of helping students identify signs, safe areas and people, and recognize potential hazards in the community.

Materials:

Large sheets of art paper (one per group), scrap paper for planning and practice, and colored marking pens

Directions:

A good way to begin this activity is to take the students on a walk through the neighborhood around the school. Point out signs, intersections, traffic lights, busy driveways — anything that is either potentially hazardous or increases safety.

When you return to the classroom, form small groups and ask the students to work together to develop a map of the neighborhood they just visited. (If you did not take the walk, spend some time reminding the students about the buildings and other features that surround the school.)

Distribute the scrap paper, art paper, and colored marking pens. Suggest that the students work individually at first, on scrap paper, and then combine their impressions and ideas to create the final map. Circulate and assist, as necessary. Help the students properly label structures and streets.

Ask each group to come forward and show its finished map to the class. Point to first one spot on the map and then another, each time asking the group to trace a route from that point to a safe location nearby. Ask questions such as:

— If you were here and something happened, where could you go to find an adult to help you?
— What helpers (police, crossing guards, storekeepers, etc.) might you find in this area?
— Why did you choose this route instead of that route?

After every group has had an opportunity to share its map, display all of the maps around the room. Facilitate a summary discussion.

Discussion Questions:

1. What makes a place safe or unsafe?
2. What are some unsafe things that kids sometimes do going to and from school?
3. What safety cautions should you remember when it's raining?
4. What kinds of areas should you stay away from?
5. Why is it better to walk or ride your bike in the company of friends?
6. What should you do if someone frightens or threatens you?

Variations:

After the map sharing and discussion about safe routes, give the students some additional time to add these routes to their maps. Suggest that they draw stick figures and print captions explaining their safety people and routes.

Safely Home Alone

A Counselor Activity

Overall Purpose:

The purpose of this activity is threefold, allowing you to present safety guidelines to latchkey children and their parents, to offer the children an opportunity to voice some of their concerns and fears, and to identify any students whose at-home situations warrant further investigation or intervention.

Materials:

One copy of the experience sheet, *Safely Home Alone*, for each student

Directions:

Ask the students how many of them have seen the movie/video, "Home Alone." Undoubtedly several students will respond in the affirmative. For the sake of those who have not seen the movie, ask a volunteer to briefly describe what it is about. Then ask: *Do things like that really happen to kids when they're home alone?*

Clarify the fact that predicaments such as Macauley Culkin encounters in his movies are exaggerated fantasies which are supposed to entertain people. In real life, such things rarely happen. In your own words, elaborate:

Being home alone is a big responsibility. And even though no one is making a movie of your life, there are some lessons to learn from Macauley Culkin. He's a smart kid who seems prepared for almost anything. We're going to talk about some ways that you can be smart and prepared, too.

Distribute the experience sheets and go over them with the students. Talk about each item on the list. Suggest that the students take the sheets home and share them with their parents. Then, in your own words, say:

Enough about Macauley Culkin. Let's talk about you. What do you worry about when you're home alone?

Encourage the students to voice any fears, uncertainties, or resentments they have. Listen and accept what the students say, offering suggestions where appropriate. Reassure the students and reinforce the notion that they are skillful, capable people. Try to end the discussion on a positive note.

Discussion Questions:

1. What does it mean to be prepared?
2. Did you get any ideas today about things you should know how to do? What are you going to do to get the answers you need?
3. Who can you talk to here at school if you feel worried about being at home alone?
4. Besides taking care of things at home, what are some other ways that you are capable?

Safety Tips for Being Home Alone

Student Experience Sheet

Almost everyone is home alone sometimes. And if both of your parents work, you may find yourself home alone often. That's okay. Scary things don't happen to most kids the way they happen in the movies. Still, you need to know how to stay safe. Read the list below. How many of these things do you know?

Do you know:

- Your full name, address, and phone number, including area code?

- Your parents' full names, the exact name of the places at which they work, and their work telephone numbers?

- How to use cell phones or land line phones to dial 911?

- How to carry a key so it is secure but out of sight?

- A safe place to go if something, such as a door ajar or a broken window, seems wrong when you get home?

- How to lock the door after you get home, and how to keep the doors and windows locked?

- Whom to go to if you are being followed?

- How to check in with your parents or a neighbor at a regularly scheduled time?

- How to avoid walking home from school alone and how to be alert and watchful if you have no one to walk with?

- How to answer the telephone without letting callers know that you are alone?

- How to get out of the house safely and quickly in case of fire?

If there's something on this list that you don't do, or don't know how to do, talk it over with your parents today.

IT FEELS GOOD TO BE PREPARED AND CAPABLE!

Centering and Balancing
A Counselor/Teacher Activity

Overall Purpose:

In this activity the students identify and label stressful situations associated with strong negative emotions and experience simple meditation exercises that can be used to relieve stress and regain emotional balance. Invite the teacher to participate fully in this activity.

Materials:

Soothing music for the music meditation

Directions:

Begin this activity by talking with the students about what it means to be out of balance. Start with bodily examples, which the students will relate to immediately, then move the discussion toward emotions. For example, ask: *How many of you have ever lost your balance?*

Ask two or three volunteers to demonstrate what happened when they lost their balance. Establish the concept of a *center* around which weight is distributed evenly when we are in balance, and that getting *off balance* usually means that too much weight has shifted to one side or another.

Then, in your own words, explain: *Losing our balance in gymnastics, walking along a wall, riding a bike, or skating are examples that occur on the <u>outside</u>, with our bodies. But we can get out of balance <u>inside</u>, too. One way we can get out of balance inside is from strong negative emotions. If we get very nervous or angry or afraid, we start to feel and act out of control or unbalanced. Can you think of a time when you were out of balance because of negative feelings?*

Invite several students to share experiences in which they felt controlled by negative emotions. List the emotions they mention on the board. Then explain further:

To get back in balance, we have to become centered again. Being centered inside means being quiet, calm, relaxed, and alert. Today, we're going to practice some simple exercises that will help us become centered.

Lead the students in one or more of the following exercises. When you have finished, facilitate a summary discussion, using the questions below. Provide the teacher with a copy of the three meditations, and encourage him or her to lead the students in at least one of the centering exercises whenever they feel stressed or out of balance.

Simple Meditation

Tell the students to sit comfortably and close their eyes. Then, slowly read this centering exercise in a soothing tone:

Take several deep breaths . . . Feel your body begin to relax. . . Breathe in and hold it . . . breathe out. . . Breathe in and hold it . . . breathe out. . . Focus your attention on your feet. . . Breathe in so deeply that you can feel the air move through your body . . . all the way to your toes. . . Do that again . . . this time feel the air sweeping all the tension and negative feelings with it . . . Breathe out . . . releasing the tension . . . pushing out the negative feelings. . . Feel your body relax more and more with each breath. . . Feel your stomach relax . . . your heart . . . your chest . . . your shoulders . . . Keep breathing . . . deeply . . . until all of the tension has left your body. . . Then, when you are ready, bring your awareness back to this room and open your eyes.

Visual Meditation

Ask the students to pick out an object somewhere in the room and go sit near it. (It's okay if several students pick the same object, just as long as they can all gather around it without crowding one another. Explain that the object can be a book, ball, picture, flower, light fixture, etc. When all of the students have picked an object and are settled, say to them:

Focus all of your attention on the object... Fix your eyes on it... Without looking away, begin to breathe deeply and slowly... Slowly and deeply... Let your body relax... Let your arms relax... let your shoulders relax... let your legs and feet relax... As you look at this object, begin to feel its energy... the energy that gives it shape ... and color... the energy that attracted you to it... Let yourself connect with the energy in this object... Let any tension or negative feelings that you have flow out of you... and into this object... Keep breathing deeply... while you watch the tension leave you. .. and flow in a stream... across space... and into the object... Send all of it there... and relax... relax... relax............. ... When you are completely relaxed, look away from the object and come back to this room.

Music Meditation

Bring some relaxing classical or new age music with you to class. Tell the students to sit comfortably and close their eyes. Begin playing the music at a low volume while you give these directions:

Take several deep breaths... and, as you listen to the music... begin to relax your body... Relax your feet and legs... Relax your stomach and back... relax your chest... relax your arms and shoulders... relax your neck... and relax all the features of your face....... Now, breathe deeply... and imagine that you are breathing in the music... breathing it into your lungs... where it enters your blood... carried by millions of molecules of oxygen... to all parts of your body... Feel the music as it flows through your arms... and hands... to the tips of your fingers... Feel it flow through your heart... your stomach... into your legs... and your feet... all the way to your toes... Let the music wash away any last bit of tension left in your body... Feel it swirl over and around any negative feelings... and carry them away... Negative feelings have no power against this music... They simply disappear....... ...... so let them go....... and when they are all gone... open your eyes... and come back to this room.

Discussion Questions:

1. How did you feel when you were doing these relaxation exercises? How did you feel immediately afterwards?
2. Why is it important to stay in balance, or get back in balance when you are stressed?
3. When you feel stressed or upset, what happens to your ability to study and learn?
4. How might you use exercises like this on your own, at school or at home?

The Stress Basket
A Counselor Activity

Overall Purpose:

This activity gives students an opportunity to identify stressful situations in their lives and to demonstrate control over them by symbolically throwing them away.

Materials:

Three small pieces of paper and a pencil for each student; a waste basket or wicker basket

Directions:

Have the students gather in one large circle. Stand in the center of the circle and, while your words ask this question, use your body and face to act it out: *When stress and bad feelings get big and heavy and start weighing you down, do you ever wish you could just throw them away?*

As you field the students' responses, go get the basket and place it in the center of the circle. Then say: *Well, today we're going to do just that!*

Give each student three small pieces of paper and a pencil. Tell the students to think of three things that cause them stress, or make them feel bad (hurt, lonely, sad, scared, etc.). Have them write one stressful thing on each piece of paper. (Give examples, as necessary.)

Start off the exercise by sharing what you have written on one of your pieces of paper. Explain the nature of your stressful situation and how it makes you feel. Then announce that you are going to get rid of this stress by throwing it away. Ceremoniously wad up the piece of paper and, without moving from your seat in the circle, throw it in the basket while saying something like, "Goodbye and good riddance!"

Go around the circle and have each student share a stressful item, wad it up, and throw it in the basket while making some kind of assertive farewell statement. After everyone has shared once, go around a second time, and a third.

Insist that the students listen attentively as each person speaks, but keep the tone of the activity light. Conclude with a summary discussion.

Discussion Questions:

1. What similarities did you hear in the stressful things we shared?
2. What kinds of feelings do stressful events and conditions cause most of us to have?
3. How did you feel when you "threw away" each stressful item?
4. What else can you do to reduce the stress that these things cause you?

Variations:

As an alternative to writing, have younger students draw a picture of a stressful situation. Don't give them time to make the picture elaborate; if they get too attached to the drawing, they might not want to throw it away.

Stress Breaks

Counselor/Teacher Activities

Overall Purpose:

To reduce stress in children by engaging them in soothing fantasies and movement exercises. In addition to the stress management techniques provided in the next activity, *De-Stressing the Test*, these are quick strategies that can be used by the teacher in the classroom to relax students before tests or anytime they are feeling tense or anxious.

Directions:

Research has demonstrated that high levels of stress actually shut down the functioning of critical portions of the brain and interfere significantly with learning. And even young children experience varying degrees of stress due to feelings and anxieties generated by family and school events.

Here are several quick techniques for relieving tension and stress and quieting tense "uptight" children. Demonstrate these techniques in the classroom and encourage teachers to use them whenever tensions and anxieties are noticeably high.

Hand Squeezing:

Join the children in a single large circle, holding hands. Tell everyone to be very quiet and concentrate very hard, because you are going to send a message around the circle. Gently squeeze the hand of the child next to you for 2-3 seconds, and whisper to the child to squeeze the hand of the next child. After the squeeze has traveled all the way around the circle, lead the children in one or two group squeezes.

Something Soft

Get the attention of the children and say to them: *Be very still. Think of something soft — the softest thing you've ever felt. Don't say what it is. Just picture it in your mind. I'm going to come around and look at each one of you, and I'll see the softness in your face.*

Fantasy Character

Create a fantasy character who occasionally visits the class. When tensions are high, surprise the children by opening the door and inviting the character in for a seat and some conversation. Ask the character questions and respond to his or her "answers." Invite the children to do the same.

Movement Exercises

- Lead the children in picking oranges from a tree, stretching up to reach each piece of fruit, stretching higher for the "biggest, juiciest piece of all," and bending down to place each piece in a bag on the floor.

- Have the children stand apart and move their arms like windmills while taking in a deep breath and holding it. Then have them reverse the direction of their arms and blow the air out in a long whoooosh! Repeat several times, slowing the speed of the windmills "on a calm, sunny afternoon" and increasing the speed, "on a windy, stormy day."

- Take a fantasy canoe trip down an alpine river. Have the children paddle left and right in unison. Have them stop and look around as you describe the scenery. Then resume paddling. Throw an anchor over in a shady inlet and rest.

- Seated in a circle, lead the group in several repetitions of an isolated movement, such as stretching the neck from side to side, moving the arms or the legs in different ways, or bending down to touch the floor in front of the chair. After the children get the idea, let them think of movements and take turns leading the group.

De-Stressing the Test

A Counselor/Teacher Activity

Overall Purpose:

This activity helps students learn to identify the physical and psychological effects of test anxiety and compare imagined consequences of failure with realistic consequences. They also will learn stress-reduction techniques that can be used to reduce test anxiety.

Materials:

One copy of the experience sheet, *How to Handle Test Anxiety,* for each student

Directions:

Begin by discussing the concept of test anxiety. Ask the students how much they worry about upcoming tests, the extent to which their lives are disrupted by test anxiety, and how they usually handle it.

At some point in the discussion, ask: *What is the absolute worst thing that could happen if you didn't do well on a test?* Encourage the students to describe the most extreme consequences they can think of. Then ask, *Okay, now that we've imagined the very worst, what do you think would really happen?*

Contrast the differences between the students' imaginings and their reality.

Next, explain to the students that some test anxiety is normal and usually not a problem. It's a type of *performance* fear—like feeling nervous before making a speech or playing in a music recital. It can help focus your mind and improve performance.

Extreme anxiety, on the other hand, can be debilitating. Chemicals released by the brain can block memory and result in a lower score. That's why it's important to learn ways to control stress levels, particularly at test time.

Ask the students to recall a recent test situation and describe how they felt just before the test. Write their contributions on the board. Include feelings such as:
- Scared
- Annoyed
- Confident
- Jittery
- Relaxed
- Paralyzed

Point out that the emotions experienced during extreme test anxiety are usually not reality-based. They are better suited to a natural disaster than they are to a test. That is why it's so important to learn and practice stress-reduction skills.

Distribute the experience sheets and go over the stress-reduction strategies with the students. Elaborate on each one and generate additional suggestions from the group. In particular, spend time discussing and practicing number 7. "Take Deep Breaths." This is a valuable, proven method of stress reduction for any circumstance. By involving the teacher in this activity, he or she can have the children practice deep breathing on a regular basis and remind them to use it prior to, and during, tests.

Discussion Questions:

1. Why is it important to get lots of sleep the night before a test? To eat healthy food?
2. What messages can you give yourself (self talk) to help reduce test anxiety?
3. What is deep breathing? When should you use deep breathing?
4. What's the best way to make sure you do well on tests?
5. What should you do if you don't understand a test question?
6. Is it okay to guess if you don't know the answer? Why or why not?
7. Which methods of reducing test stress do you already use?
8. What new method do you plan to try?

How to Handle Test Anxiety

Student Experience Sheet

**Having a test? Don't let stress ruin your day – or your score.
Take these steps to lower stress.**

1. **Prepare.** Read. Do your homework. Ask questions. Enjoy learning. If you do these things, your test scores will be fine.

2. **Get lots of sleep.** Your brain and body need rest. Sleep at least eight hours the night before a test.

3. **Eat healthy food.** Good food makes for a good performance. Skip the sugary snacks. Eat nuts and fruits instead, and don't forget to eat breakfast.

4. **Think positive.** Tell yourself that you are going to do exceptionally well on the test. Avoid negative, discouraging thoughts. Focus your thoughts on being ready, relaxed, and confident.

5. **Picture success.** Imagine yourself calmly taking the test and remembering everything you need to know. Have this daydream often.

6. **Ask for help.** If you still get very nervous before tests, talk it over with your teacher or counselor. They can help.

7. **Take deep breaths.** Deep breathing really helps your body to relax. Whenever you are feeling tense or anxious, either before or during a test, stop and take several deep breaths in through your nose, holding it for a moment and then slowly exhale out through your mouth. Make sure you can feel your stomach rise when you breath in. That's how you know it's really deep breathing. Practice your deep breathing often and use it during stressful moments.

Which method of stress reduction have you used? _____

_____

_____

What new method will you try? _____

_____

_____

Many Paths: An Exercise in Critical Thinking

A Counselor Activity

Overall Purpose:

This activity gives students repeated opportunities to experience the power of focused, critical thinking; demonstrates that there are many possible solutions to a single problem or paths to a single goal; and encourages creativity.

Materials:

Timer or clock/watch with a second hand; a list of topics (see below) written on the board or a chart prior to the session; writing materials for the recorder in each small group

Directions:

Tell the students that you have come to visit today to ask their help in doing some critical thinking.

Ask the students how many know what brainstorming is. Listen to the comments of those who have participated in brainstorming sessions before, and clarify that brainstorming is a process in which many ideas or solutions are generated for solving a problem or handling a situation. In your own words, explain further, using an example:

Imagine that you and a friend want to surprise another friend by doing something special on his or her birthday. There are many possible things that you could do, but until you think of them, you can't choose them. The more ideas you come up with, the better your chances of choosing the perfect surprise. You decide to hold a brainstorming session. You spend 5 minutes listing as many ideas as you can think of. You write them all down, and you don't stop to discuss any of them until the 5 minutes are up. You just keep thinking and throwing out ideas. Afterwards you go back and talk about each idea, and then agree on the best one.

Ask the students if they can help you make a list of rules for brainstorming, based on the process you just described. You should end up with these rules on the board:

1. Suggest as many ideas as you can think of. Don't worry about details, just be creative.
2. Write down every idea.
3. Don't reject, put down, evaluate or discuss any idea during the brainstorming process.

Have the students form small groups of four or five and choose a recorder. Make sure that the recorders have paper and pencils. Then, in your own words, explain the assignment:

Pick a topic from the list I've prepared. I will give you the signal to start brainstorming. You will have 3 minutes to come up with as many ideas as you can think of. Write them all down, and be sure to follow the rules. At the end of 3 minutes, I'll give you the signal to stop.

Circulate and observe the groups. Call time at the end of 3 minutes. Do a quick check of each group, commenting on the number of ideas generated, reinforcing the students for their creativity. Review any rules that the students had difficulty with.

If possible, have the groups repeat the process several more times, using new topics during each round. Do not evaluate (or allow the students to evaluate) any suggested ideas. Focus entirely on gaining practice in brainstorming. Reserve about 10 minutes for a culminating class discussion.

Discussion Questions:

1. What was easiest about brainstorming? What was hardest?
2. Why is it important to think of many different possibilities when you are trying to solve a problem?
3. Why not just do the first thing that pops into your head?
4. Once you have a long list of ideas, what do you do next?

Topics:

- What can you do to help out at home?
- How can you surprise your parent on her/his birthday?
- How can you make your room a better place to study?
- What can you do to have fun on a rainy Saturday?
- What can you do if you get lost?
- What can you do if you think someone is following you?
- How can we rearrange the classroom to make it different?
- What kind of a class party shall we have for the holidays?
- How can we show our thanks as a class on Thanksgiving?
- How can we make the school more attractive?
- How can you meet and make new friends?
- How can we decide who goes first in a game?
- How can we design a better playground?

Variations:

When working with younger students, conduct the brainstorming sessions with the total group, facilitating and writing ideas on the board.

Making Decisions
A Counselor/Teacher Activity

Overall Purpose:

This activity increases student awareness of the number of decisions they make every day, and of the processes and relative risks involved in each one. In addition, students are given a list of steps to follow when making important, conscious decisions.

Materials:

One copy of the experience sheet, Decisions, Decisions!, for each student

Directions:

Ask a volunteer to come up to the front of the class. Ask the student to describe everything he/she did the day before. Note on the board all decision points, *e.g.*, got up (whether to get up), ate breakfast (what to eat), got dressed (what to wear), etc. Chances are the student will give a very limited version of his or her activities, so be prepared to question and probe a little for more decision points.

Once you have a list of decisions on the board, ask every member of the class to take out a piece of paper and write down the three most important decisions (from the list), in order of importance. Give the students about 2 minutes to do this. Then go through the list with them. Point to each item and ask for a show of hands from students who thought that item was "most important." Tally the numbers and record them next to the item. Go through the list two more times, tallying "second most important" and "third most important."

Take the "most important" decision and ask your volunteer a series of questions: *How did you decide (what to eat, what to wear, what to read, etc.)?*

Through further questions and discussion, make these points about decision making (geared to the age/sophistication of the group):

- Before you can make a decision, you have to have choices.
- Decision making is the process of deciding from among choices.
- How you choose is based on what you know and what you like or value.

   In order to have a choice between cereal and pancakes, you have to know that both are available. At home, you find out by asking or looking. At a restaurant, you find out by reading the menu. Then you choose what sounds best. Or, if time is short, you may choose the cereal even though you like pancakes better (a values decision).

- Every decision involves some level of risk.

   If you decide on pancakes even though time is short, you risk missing the school bus. If you decide on cereal, you may feel dissatisfied, not finish your breakfast, and have hunger pangs all morning.

- Some decisions require study and careful thought. Other decisions are made very quickly, with almost no conscious thought at all.
- The more important a decision, the more time you should give it —usually.
- The more you know about yourself —what your goals are, what you like and value —the more likely you are to make a good decision (the lower the risk).

Distribute the experience sheets. Go through the decision-making steps with the students, tying the process into your earlier discussion. Remind the students to fill out the decision log. Tell them when to bring it back to class.

After the students have completed and returned their decision log, lead a summary discussion.

If you cannot return to class to facilitate the follow-up session, ask the teacher to talk to the students about their decision logs and lead the final discussion using the discussion questions provided and any additional questions he or she can come up with.

Discussion Questions:

1. What kinds of decisions did you make most often, small ones or big ones?
2. How often did you try to follow the decision-making steps? How was it?
3. How many of your decisions were made because someone told you to make them? Did you still have choices?
4. Why is it important to get information when you have an important decision to make?
5. What have you learned about decision making from this activity?

Decisions, Decisions!

Student Experience Sheet

Every day, you make many decisions. Some are big decisions, and some are so small that you hardly think about them. But, even with small decisions, your brain goes through certain steps. Here they are. You may find this list helpful the next time you make a big decision.

Steps for Making a Decision

1. Describe the decision that needs to be m
2. Gather information
2. List all of your choices.
3. Study the choices
4. Decide which choice is best.
5. Put your choice into action.

How do YOU make decisions?

Every time you decide to spend your time doing one thing instead of another, you are making a decision. Keep track of all your decisions this weekend. Use the chart on the next page. Your counselor or teacher will tell you when to bring this sheet back to class.

118

Decision Log

	Decision	Time	Did you have choices?	Did you think about your choice?	Are you satisfied with your choice?
Day 1					
Day 2					

Dear Class... Practice in Problem Solving

A Counselor/Teacher Activity

Overall Purpose:

Use this activity to familiarize students with a problem-solving process, and to give them opportunities to generate and evaluate solutions to hypothetical and real problems.

Materials:

An advice column such as "Dear Abby" (current and archived Dear Abby columns are available on the internet); 4" by 6" index cards; one copy of the experience sheet, *Problem-Solving Flow Chart,* for each student

Directions:

Bring the advice column to class. Read a typical problem to the students. Choose one that they can relate to, for example, one involving kids. Do not read the columnist's answer. Instead, ask the students: *What answer would you give to this person?*

Listen to the ideas of several students, clarifying and feeding back what you hear. Ask two or three of these students how they arrived at their solutions and note the steps (if any) on the board.

Distribute the index cards. Have the students each think of a typical problem that someone their age might have, and write it on the card as though writing to an advice columnist. Tell them to use the salutation, "Dear Class" and to sign a fictitious name like "Worried in the Back of the Room" or "Hiding Under My Desk." Collect all of the problem cards.

If you have recorded some problem-solving steps on the board, expand on them to complete a list comparable to the one below. Otherwise, present the following steps and talk briefly about each one (suggested comments are in parentheses):

Steps for Solving a Problem Responsibly

1. **Stop all blaming.** (Blaming is a waste of time and energy and does not help solve the problem.)

2. **Define the problem.** (Try to describe all parts of the problem. You can't solve something that you don't understand.)

3. **Consider asking for help.** (Some problems can't be solved alone. Would it help to talk this over with someone you trust?)

4. **Think of possible solutions.** (Think of as many as you can. You may need to get more information in order to do this.)

5. **Evaluate the solutions.** (Ask yourself, *What will happen to me and others if I choose this one?*)

6. **Choose a solution.** (Pick the one that has the best chance of working. It doesn't have to be perfect.)

7. **Implement the solution.** (This takes planning. Decide what steps to take, as well as how and when to take them.)

8. **Ask yourself,** *Did my solution work?* (Is the problem gone? If so, it worked. If not, pick a different solution and try again.)

Ask the students to keep these steps in mind as they discuss solutions to the problems you are about to read. Randomly choose one of the cards and read it aloud. Act as a facilitator as the students discuss the problem and possible solutions. Guide them through the steps, when appropriate, up to and including step #6. Bring closure to the discussion by asking the class to choose one solution to recommend. If the students are able to agree, ask someone to write the solution on the back of the card. Set the card aside.
Repeat this procedure with additional cards, as time allows. During the last few minutes of the session, lead a summary discussion. Leave the experience sheets with the teacher for distribution at the end of the day or on a follow-up day.

Discussion Questions:

1. What did you learn from solving other people's problems?
2. Why is it important to define a problem correctly?
3. When do you think a kid should ask for help in solving a problem?
4. How difficult was it to come up with several possible solutions to these problems?
5. Why is it important to have choices?
6. If a solution doesn't work, what should you do?
7. How is this process like the one you use to solve your own problems? How is it different?

Variations:

Return to the class for additional sessions, continuing the process described. At about your third session with the same group, ask the students to submit real problems, anonymously. If you cannot return to the class regularly, ask the teacher to assume the role of facilitator.

Save all of the problems that are "solved" by the group (each with a solution written on the back). Keep these cards in a basket or box at a "Problem-Solving Center."

Problem-Solving Flow Chart
Student Experience Sheet

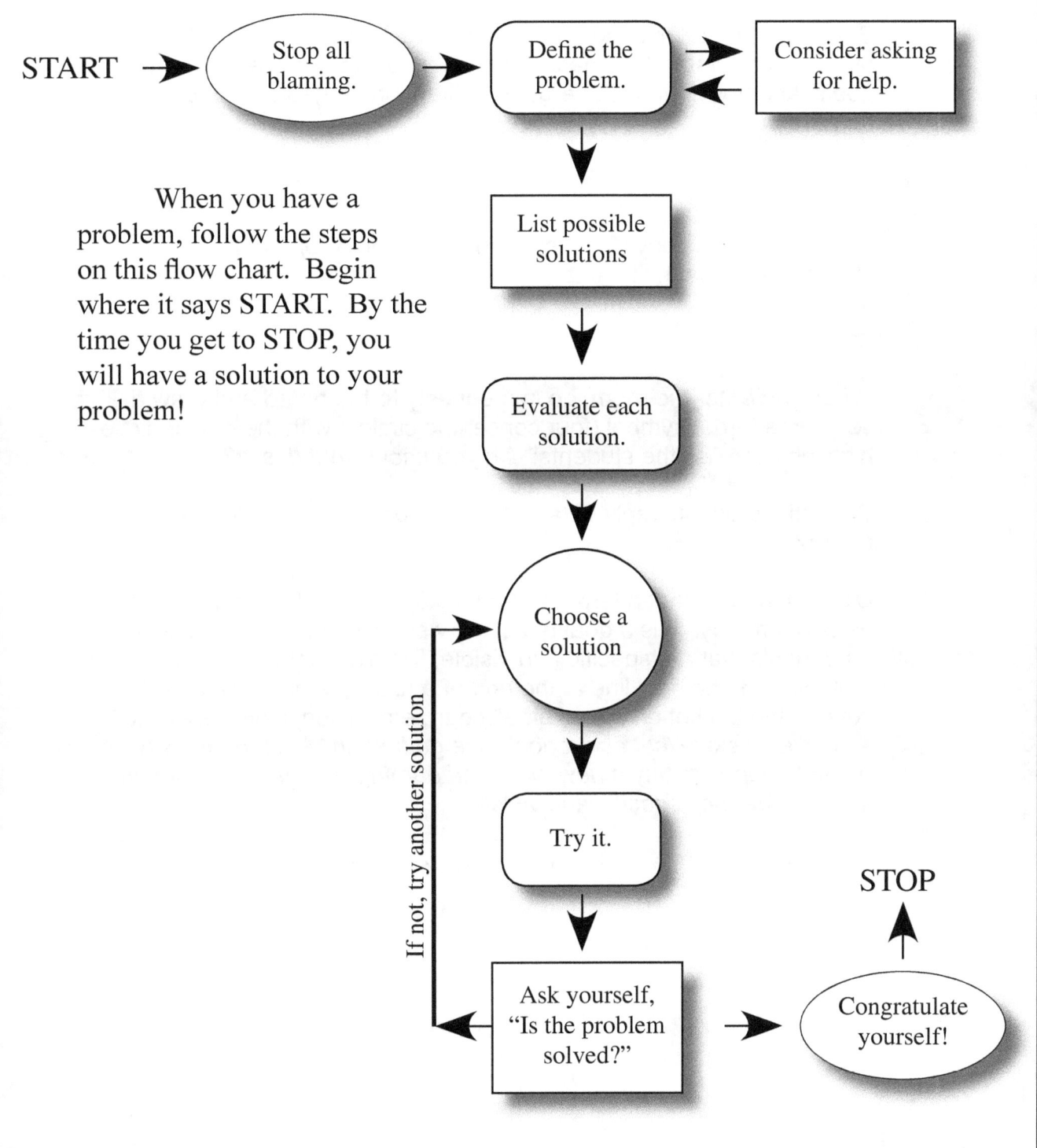

When you have a problem, follow the steps on this flow chart. Begin where it says START. By the time you get to STOP, you will have a solution to your problem!

Targeting Short-Term Goals
A Counselor Activity

Overall Purpose:

Starting with a comparison of goals to targets, this activity helps students understand the nature of goals, how to formulate short-term goals, and how to focus energy and attention on goals in order to achieve them.

Materials:

Pencils and one copy of the experience sheet, *Keep Your Eye on Your Goal,* for each student

Directions:

When you enter the room, go immediately to the board and draw a very large target symbol (four concentric circles, with the center circle highlighted). Ask the students: *Do you know what this is?*

When the students reply, *a target*, ask: *...and what exactly is a target?*

Discuss the fact that a target is something you aim for when you play darts or archery. It is a goal that is very specific and visible. Name other goals that are specific and visible, like the goal posts on a football field, the goal line at the end of a race, the holes on a golf course, the basket on a basketball court, etc. Then, using relevant examples, ask: *What about goals like getting an "A" on a test, saving enough money to buy a new bike, and earning a particular badge in scouts. Are they specific and visible?*

Write each example on the board and examine it with the students.

Establish that to make the first goal specific, you have to name the exact test and the day of the test. To make the second goal specific, you have to know which bike you want to buy and how much it costs, and to make the third goal specific, you have to decide which badge you want to earn. Write these details into the goal statements and draw a target next to each one. Say: Now these goals are just like targets. They are specific, and they are visible because we can see them in our minds.

Next, ask the students: When you want to hit a target, what do you look at — the pretty scenery in the distance or the faces in the bleachers?

You will get a resounding "no," and the students will clearly convey that you have to focus on the target. Take advantage of this moment and ask the students how they would focus on getting the "A," on saving money for the bike, and on earning the badge. Help them articulate that they would spend significant time doing things that would help them reach the goal.

Distribute the student experience sheets and go over the directions. Model the process for the students by setting three goals for yourself. Write them in the target symbol you have drawn on the board. Demonstrate how goals are written by making yours:
- positive
- stated in the present tense ("I organize my desk.")
- realistic
- within your control

Explain the importance of each one of these guidelines, and then give the students about 10 minutes to write their goals. Have the students share their goals with a partner and suggest that they keep them in the front of their notebook or tape them to a mirror or bulletin board at home. Lead a culminating discussion.

Discussion Questions:

1. How does goal setting help you get things done?
2. Why is it important to set goals that are realistic?
3. What are some ways to remind yourself of your goals, besides writing them down?
4. How can you reward yourself when you reach your goals?

Variations:

Have younger students formulate one goal. With the teacher's assistance, circulate and help the students write down their goal. Simplify all explanations and directions.

Keep An Eye on Your Goal!
Student Experience Sheet

A goal is a target. In order to hit it, you have to look at it, think about it, and do the things that move you toward it.

Think of three things that you want to accomplish this week. These are your goals. Write each goal in one of the spaces on the target.

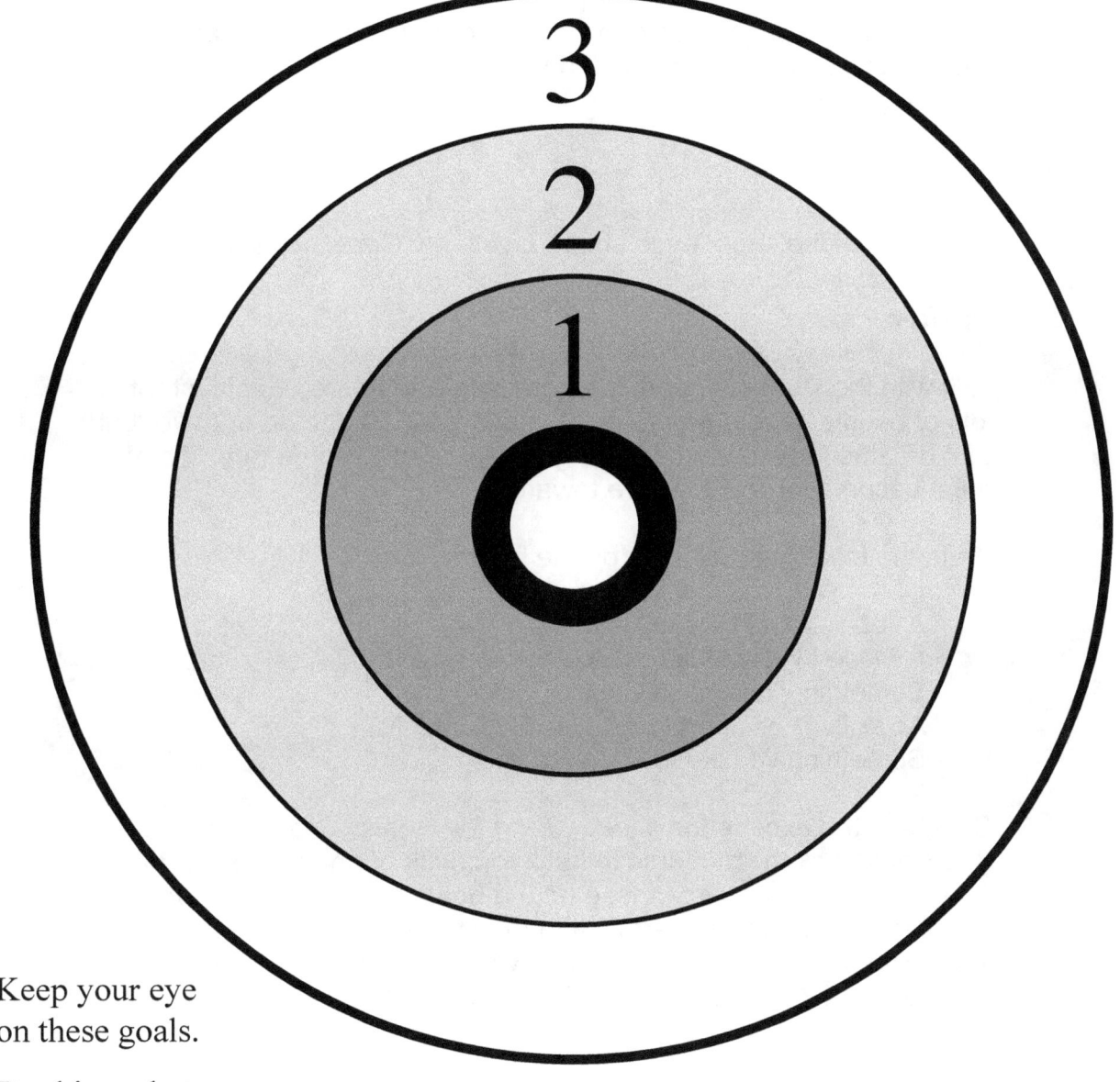

Keep your eye on these goals.

Do things that move you toward them. At the end of the week, give yourself 25 points for each goal you reach.

Write the total in the center of the target.

Charting the Future: Individual Goal Setting

A Counselor/Teacher Activity

Overall Purpose:

This activity allows students to set long range goals, to visualize themselves achieving a goal, and to write a creative story about its accomplishment.

Materials:

One copy of the experience sheet, *Living My Goals,* for each student

Directions:

Talk with the students about their goals for the future. Explain that lots of people have dreams about things they want to do or have, but that dreams must be turned into goals in order to come true. They must become targets to move toward.

Write the following headings on the board:

- A Job I Would Like to Have
- A Place I Would Like to Go
- Something I'd Like to Own
- An Activity or Sport I'd Like To Be Good At
- Something I'd Like to Accomplish

Distribute the experience sheet, *Living My Goals,* and review the directions. Ask the students to help you think of an example or two for each goal area. Write these on the board under the appropriate headings. Once you're certain that the students have grasped the idea, give them about 10 minutes to work on their goals. You and the teacher should circulate and assist the students in formulating their goals.

At the end of 10 minutes (use your judgment in allowing more or less time), invite volunteers to share their goals with the group.

Then, in your own words, say to the students:

Turn your papers over. Imagine that time has passed, and the future is here. You are achieving one of your goals. Picture it happening in your mind and describe what you see in the form of a story. Use your imagination and be very specific. Describe your feelings and why reaching this goal is so important to you.

Give the students another 15 minutes to write. As time permits, invite individual students to read their stories to the class. Applaud each story and its author. Ask the teacher to display the stories around the room. Lead a summary discussion.

Discussion Questions:

1. How do we benefit from setting goals for the future?
2. What similarities did you hear in the goals we wrote?
3. When is it okay to change your mind about a goal?
4. Should you change your mind about a goal just because it takes hard work? Why or why not?
5. How will you know that you are getting closer to your goal?

Variations:

Teacher Activity: Set up a "Goal Center" in the room. Hang a sign over it and display the completed experience sheets there. Set out a stack of 3" by 5" cards and pencils so that the students can write additional short-term and long range goals. Locate childrens' literature and games related to goal-setting and keep them at the center.

Living My Goals
Student Experience Sheet

A goal is something you work for, move toward, and finally reach. When you have goals, you know exactly where you're going.

Describe 5 goals. When you have finished, turn this sheet over and write a story about one of your goals on the back. Imagine that you are achieving your goal. Describe what it's like and how you feel.

A Job I Would Like to Have _____
_____
_____

A Place I Would Like to Go _____
_____
_____

Something I'd Like to Own _____
_____
_____

An Activity or Sport I'd Like To Be Good At _____
_____
_____

Something I'd Like to Accomplish _____
_____
_____

Words to Grow On

A Counselor Activity

Overall Purpose:

This activity introduces the concept of self-talk. Use it to help students become aware of positive and negative words and phrases they typically use in talking to themselves and others, and to have them experience the effects of those words through humorous demonstrations.

Directions:

Begin by asking the students what they need in order to grow. They will answer food, perhaps naming specific foods like milk and vegetables. Some might say they need air to breathe and some might even say love. Accept and acknowledge the accuracy of what the students say. Then, tell them that you have in mind something else that makes people grow — words. In your own words, say:

Yes, it's true. Positive words actually make us bigger. We stand straighter, look taller, feel better, and act older when we hear positive words about ourselves. And it doesn't matter if someone else says those words to us or we say them to ourselves. The effect is the same. Of course, the opposite is true with negative words. They make us get smaller. When people say negative things to us —or we say them to ourselves — we slump, look shorter, feel worse, and often act younger. Can you believe that words do all that?

Ask the students to help you brainstorm two lists: one made up of positive things people say, and the other made up of negative things. Get the process going by suggesting some phrases yourself and writing them on the board, under the headings, "Growing" and "Shrinking." Accept contributions from the students, and build lists that include items like:

Growing

- That's great!
- Good work!
- I like that!
- You can do that.
- You're doing a good job.
- This is fun to learn.
- That's easy.
- I'll try it.
- This is interesting.

Shrinking

- That's awful.
- Poor work!
- I hate this.
- I can't do this.
- You're doing a lousy job.
- This is a drag.
- This is too hard.
- I don't want to.
- This is boring.

Next, have some fun by demonstrating how the words and phrases work. Ask a student to read through the negative list, saying the phrases directly to you. As the student reads, start to "shrink." Visibly get smaller with each phrase, until (if willing) you are on the floor. Then (looking up from the floor) ask the student to read the list of positive words to you. Start to "grow" and get taller with each phrase. Finally, stand on a chair to make yourself as tall as possible. Ham it up. Let your facial expressions and posture reflect increasing negative/positive effects.

Have the students form dyads and take turns doing the same exercise.

When the mirth has subsided, point out that most of the negative things people hear actually come from themselves, not from others. Ask the students: *How many of you say negative things like these to yourselves?*

Explain that the things we say to ourselves make up our "self-talk," and that we need to replace negative self-talk with positive self-talk in order to grow.

Go around the room and have every student make a positive statement about him- or herself starting with the word "I." Model the process. If a student can't think of something to say, point to the board and help the student pick a phrase from the "Growing" list.

Conclude the activity with a discussion.

Discussion Questions:

1. How do you feel when someone makes a "growing" statement to you?
2. How do you feel when someone makes a "shrinking" statement to you?
3. Which is easier, saying negative things to ourselves or saying positive things? Why?
4. How do we learn our self-talk habits?
5. How can we help each other use positive self-talk?
6. What are some "growing" words you can say to yourself?

Strength Bombardment
A Counselor/Teacher Activity

Overall Purpose:

This activity helps students become more aware of their own strengths and those of others, and provides a structured forum in which students hear numerous positive statements about themselves, and practice giving them to each other.

Materials:

Chart paper and markers, a small pad of self-sticking labels, a pencil, and a large sheet of plain paper for each student

Directions:

Tell the students that today you are going to focus on strengths. Ask: *Do you know what a strength is?*

Discuss the concept briefly, explaining that all people have strengths — good qualities, talents, and skills that others like and that make them successful. Point out that there are many words which name strengths, and ask the students to help you list some of them. On chart paper, develop a list that includes such things as:

nice	funny
handsome	good sport
generous	honest
kind	plays the piano well
runs fast	writes great stories
good in Math	smart
friendly	loyal
pretty hair	

Distribute the labels and pencils. Have every student label one sticker for each person in the class, by writing the person's first name and last initial on the sticker. You and the teacher should participate in this, too.

Instruct the students to go back through their stickers and write a positive statement on each one. Tell them to think about the person, look at the list of strengths on the chart, and describe a quality or ability that they like in that person. Allow plenty of time for this phase of the activity.

Give each student a plain piece of paper. Tell the students to write their name at the top.

Gather the class in a single large circle and explain the strength bombardment exercise. In your own words, say:

One person at a time passes his or her sheet of paper around the circle. When the sheet comes to you, find the label you have made for that person and stick it on the sheet. Then look at the person, say his or her name, and describe the strength. You might say, *Ted, the strength I see in you is your humor*. When it's your turn to receive strength statements, just listen and accept what people tell you. You may say "thank you," but that's all.

Proceed with the strength bombardment. Afterwards, lead a brief summary discussion. Suggest that the students take their strength papers home, display them on a wall or bulletin board, and look at them often.

Discussion Questions:

1. How did you feel when you were receiving strength statements?
2. How did you feel when you were giving strength statements?
3. Why is it important to recognize our own strengths and those of others?

Variations:

- Spread the activity over two, three, or four sessions. Ask the teacher to lead interim sessions, but be present at the first — to introduce the concept — and at the last — to lead the strength bombardment. Display the list of strengths at each session.

- With older students, you may conduct the strength bombardment in smaller groups; however, the more classmates each student can hear from, the better.

Linked Together
A Counselor Activity

Overall Purpose:

In this activity, students symbolize a unique gift or talent they possess, and acknowledge the gifts and talents of other class members. They are guided to recognize the contributions of students with special needs, and to demonstrate understanding that strength exists in diversity.

Materials:

Light-weight bristol board or poster paper (sturdy, but flexible) cut into 2 by 10 strips (one per student, plus a few extras); marking pens in various colors; stapler and staples

Directions:

Ask the students to think of ways that they rely on each other in the classroom. Through discussion, illustrate how each person utilizes the gifts and talents of every other person, which enhances learning and makes school more fun. For example:
— Sue draws pictures for people.
— Manuel brings interesting things to share.
— Bobby shows us how to use the computer.
— Cindy helps us when we're stuck on a math problem.
— Dana is always in a good mood.

If there are students in the class with special needs, be sure to include them in your examples. All students offer something unique; your challenge is to know (by talking with the teacher ahead of time, perhaps) what each of these students contributes.

Move the discussion toward a more specific focus on disabilities. For example, you might say something like:

Imagine that I'm a student in the class and I have a vision loss. I can only see lights and shadows. To compensate for my vision loss, I've developed keen senses of hearing and touch. I enjoy music and I'm teaching myself to play the keyboard. I'd like to learn to use a computer. How can I assist you? How can you assist me?

Continue the discussion until you sense that the students have grasped the concept of interdependence. Then distribute the paper strips and colored marking pens.

Explain that each strip represents a link in the classroom chain. Ask the students to use the markers to print their name on the strip, and to add a small drawing or symbol that shows a talent or skill they contribute to the class. Allow about 15 minutes for this process. Encourage collaboration. Make a link for yourself, and ask the teacher to make a link, too.

Have the students join you to form one large circle. Go around the circle and ask each member to hold up his or her link and explain the meaning of the symbol or drawing. After the the first and second students share, give them the stapler and ask them to form their links into interlocking circles. After the third student shares, have that person attach his or her link to the chain. Pass the stapler to each new person who shares so that the chain grows longer and longer and is finally fastened together by the last person who shares. Hang the chain somewhere in the room. Facilitate a follow-up discussion.

Discussion Questions:

1. What does our chain stand for?
2. How does it feel to know that we are all linked together?
3. How can you let others know that you depend on them?
4. What behaviors will demonstrate that you can be depended upon?
5. What have you learned from this activity?

The Take on Tolerance

A Counselor Activity

Overall Purpose:

The mini-simulations that make up this activity allow students to confront issues of prejudice, intolerance, and exclusion in nonthreatening ways, and in the process increase their understanding of inclusion and willingness to demonstrate tolerance toward individuals and groups.

Directions:

As soon as you have the attention of the class, without explanation, say: *I want everyone with blue eyes to get up and go stand in the back of the room.*

As soon as the blue-eyed students have left the group, say something like this to the remainder of the class:

I don't like people with blue eyes. They think they're so special. Don't you agree? We don't need them in our group.

Encourage a few students to join in your derision of blue-eyed people until everyone gets the point. Then call the blue-eyed students back to their seats. Next, say: *Okay, this time everyone who wears glasses or contacts go stand in that corner over there.*

When the eye-wear students have left the group, say to the rest of the class:

People who wear glasses make me uncomfortable. Why can't they see like the rest of us?

Again, encourage comments from the class before calling the ostracized group back. Repeat the process, expelling two or three additional groups of students with commonalities like:

- Everyone wearing white socks
- Everyone with hair covering their ears
- Everyone not wearing some kind of athletic shoe.
- Everyone who speaks only one language.

Reassemble the entire class and generate discussion by asking the students to explain what you were doing and why. As the students offer their insights, write key terms on the board, such as *exclusion, inclusion, prejudice, tolerance, segregation*, etc.

Next, ask the class to think of groups of people that really do experience exclusion in our society. Write ideas on the board. Your list might include:
African Americans
Asian Americans
Native Americans
Hispanic Americans
Gays and lesbians
People with disabilities
Fat people
Poor and homeless people

Pick three groups from the list and ask the students this question: *If you had to become a member of one of these three groups, which would be your first choice, second choice, and third choice?*

Give the students a few moments, then ask volunteers to explain their decisions and reasoning to the rest of the class. Repeat the exercise with more specific choices, such as: *Who would you be if you had to choose between:*
— *Hispanic American living in East Los Angeles;*
— *Native American living on an Arizona reservation; or*
— *Person in a wheelchair job hunting in Chicago?*

Again, require volunteers to support their choices with reasoning. Facilitate discussion concerning the need to exercise tolerance toward individuals and groups that are perceived as "different." Point out that most of the differences mentioned are superficial, and emphasize that people are more alike than they are different. Use the discussion questions below, and/or others that are sparked by the contributions of students.

Discussion Questions:

1. What does "tolerance" mean?
2. How does it feel to be excluded because of something you can't change?
3. Are you more tolerant or less tolerant than other people you know? Explain.
4. How many of you would not vote for a woman for U.S. President? Why?
5. Is it okay to marry someone of a different religion or race? Why or why not?
6. What are some ways in which everyone is the same?
7. Do all of us have skin? ...hair? ...a personality? ...a family? ...favorite activities? ...a language? ...holidays? ...favorite foods?
8. What can you do to become more tolerant of others during this school year?

Variations:

If time allows, have older students form small groups (six to eight) and discuss one of the following topics:
- Something I have trouble tolerating in others
- A time someone was prejudiced against me
- A time I accepted the ideas of someone I didn't like
- A way in which I'm becoming more tolerant of others

Put-down Survey
A Counselor/Teacher Activity

Overall Purpose:

To make students aware of a common communication habit that is often hurtful to others and can damage relationships. To help students understand some of the reasons that people put others down, and empathize with the receiver of put-down statements. Note: The counselor introduces this activity and the teacher completes it.

Materials:

paper and pencils

Directions:

Counselor introduction: Tell the class that today you want to focus on a way of talking that is very common at school. Explain that talking this way often starts out as a form of joking around or teasing, and then turns into a habit that continues without thought. Unfortunately, this habit can be hurtful to others and serves no real purpose. Ask the students to guess what you're talking about. Give them a few moments and if no one guesses *put-downs or putting others down*, write the term on the board.

Ask the students to help you make a list of all the statements they remember hearing people say that put others down. As the students give you the words, write them on the board, enclosing each phrase in quotation marks, *e.g.*, "You'd forget your head if it weren't attached."

Talk about the nature of put-downs. Ask the students:
— *Why do people put each other down?*
— *Are some put-downs worse than others? Which ones?*
— *How can a person tell the difference between a put-down that is meant as a joke and a put-down that is meant as verbal abuse (is intentionally hurtful)?*

Give the students the following assignment: *For the next 24 hours, I want you to carry a pencil and a piece of paper with you and write down every put-down statement that you hear. Write down put-downs that are directed at you, and put-downs that you overhear between others. Record put-downs you hear on any TV shows or through social media, too. Bring your list to class tomorrow* (or designate another day).

Teacher follow-up: Have the students take out their put-down surveys. While you record examples on the board, go around the room and have each student read and *act out* two items from his or her list. Instruct the students to try not to repeat the substance of any previously read item, and to mimic as closely as possible the method of delivery they witnessed when they observed the put-down.

When everyone has had a turn to contribute, ask if there are any additional put-downs that should be added to the list. Then, go back and categorize and tally the examples. Here are three possible categories.
1. Reflex put-downs (result of an unconscious communication habit)
2. Teasing or joking put-downs
3. Malicious (intentionally hurtful) put-downs

Discuss the different motivations that lead to each type of put-down, emphasizing that *all* types are often interpreted by the receiver as intentionally hurtful and can damage friendships. Use the questions below to stimulate further discussion, or formulate questions of your own.

Discussion Questions:

1. How are put-downs related to abuse?
2. When do put-downs lead to physical fighting?
3. How can you respond to people who tease you? ...bully you? .... insult you?
4. How can you break the habit of putting others down?

Variations:

- Limit the number of put-downs that younger students must observe and remember. Three might be a reasonable number for a 24-hour period.

- Return to the classroom and lead the follow-up session yourself.

A Fold Apart

A Counselor Activity

Overall Purpose:

To have students identify groups of people whom they consider "like" them and "different from" them, and to explore the basis for their perceptions and the effects those perceptions have on their attitudes.

Materials:

Magazines, newspapers, and department-store catalogs; scissors and glue; one large sheet of construction paper for each student

Directions:

Put the magazines out where the students can access them. Tell the students that you want them to go through the magazines and cut out six to eight pictures of people who appear to be *different from* them.

When the students have completed the task, ask them to go back through the magazines and cut out six to eight pictures of people who appear to be *like* them.

Distribute the construction paper, scissors, and glue. Have the students fold their paper in half and label one half "Like Me" and the other half "Different from Me." Then, instruct the students to arrange and glue down the "different" pictures on one side of the fold and the "like" pictures on the other.

Circulate as the students work, engaging them in conversations about their selections. Ask questions like, *How is this person like you?,* and *How do you know that this person differs from you?*

Have the students take turns sharing their collages with the class. Encourage each child to explain how the people on the "Like Me" side of the collage are different from the people on the "Different from Me" side. Ask some of the questions listed below or generate your own. Following the discussion, display the collages on a bulletin board in the classroom.

Discussion Questions:

1. What kinds of things did most of us think made people different or the same?
2. How does it feel to be thought of as different?
3. How do we act toward people we see as different?
4. What kinds of problems does being different cause between groups of people?
5. What can individuals and groups do to understand each other better?
6. How can you include more people in your "like me" group?

The Classroom Tree
A Counselor/Teacher Activity

Overall Purpose:

To graphically represent the diversity of cultural and ethnic backgrounds in the classroom, and to help the students appreciate the benefits of diversity.

Materials:

One copy of the experience sheet, *What Are My Roots?*, for each student; four to six uniquely shaped leaf patterns; construction paper in different colors; scissors; marking pens; glue, transparent tape, or thumb tacks

Directions:

Part I can be led by the teacher.

Prepare a bulletin board by covering it with paper and drawing on it the outline of a tree, with branches extending to all corners of the board. (If you prefer, cut the stump and branches from construction paper and affix them to the board.)

Talk to the students about the wealth of different cultures, languages, and heritages that make up our society. Emphasize that one of our greatest strengths as a nation is our diversity. Point out that many communities and schools have diverse populations, too, and that the students are going to have an opportunity to demonstrate just how many different cultures and backgrounds contribute to their class.

Distribute the experience sheets and review the purpose and directions with the students. In your own words, explain: *Interview one of your parents or another adult who knows something about your family background. Ask the questions on the sheet, and carefully write down the answers that your interviewee gives. When you bring your interview form back to class, we will use the information to create a "Classroom Tree."*

Part II can be led by the counselor and teacher together.

From the completed interview forms, help the students identify a ancestral country, cultural background, or first language. Distribute the leaf patterns, colored construction paper, scissors, and marking pens. Have the students select a leaf pattern, trace it on their choice of construction paper, and cut it out. Then have the students write their ancestral descriptor on the leaf, along with their name.

Attach all of the leaves to branches of the Classroom Tree. When the tree is complete, focus the class on one leaf at a time. Ask the student whose leaf is being examined to tell the class a little about his or her family "roots."

As the children share, facilitate discussion using the questions below or some that you have generated.

Discussion Questions:

1. How did you feel when you were interviewing your family member? What new information did you learn?
2. Why is it important to know our cultural roots?
3. How do we all benefit from the cultural diversity in our classroom?
4. Why do some people act as though everyone should be like them?
5. What can we do to help others appreciate diversity?

Variations:

- For younger students, modify the interview form to include a note to parents, asking their help in completing the form.

- Use one color and/or leaf shape to represent languages, another to represent ancestral countries, and a third for other kinds of descriptors. Cluster the leaves by type on different branches of the tree.

What Are My Roots?

Student Experience Sheet

All of us have family roots. If we trace our families back far enough, we can learn about our ancestors. Talk to a parent or other family member. Write down his or her answers to the questions below.

1. What is our family's first language? _____
   _____

2. In what countries did our ancestors live? _____
   _____

3. When did our family first come to the United States? _____
   _____

4. What else can you tell me about my family roots? _____
   _____
   _____
   _____
   _____
   _____

Bring your completed experience sheet to class and share what you learned!

Good or Bad? Teaching Ethics

A Counselor Activity

Overall Purpose:

This activity encourages students to evaluate their own and others' behavior, to share and discuss different perceptions of the same behavior, to recognize the difference between "thinking about" and "doing," and to consider how a person's values and ethics are formed.

Materials:

Chart paper, marking pens, masking tape, and three signs prepared prior to the session (see below)

Directions:

Ask the students if they know what the term ethics means. Write the word on the board, listen to any ideas that the students voice, and clarify that ethics are principles or values having to do what is right and wrong.

Ask the students: *Who can tell us about something you've done in the last few days that was a good thing to do?*

Call on volunteers. After each person shares, ask him or her: *How did you know that what you did was a good thing to do?*

Discuss various ways of knowing: because it feels good, because parents have said it's good, because anything else would feel bad, etc.

Next, ask the students: *Who would like to tell us about a bad thing you've done recently?*

Again, ask each volunteer: *How do you know that what you did was bad?*

Be sure to take a turn yourself and share something that you're not proud of having done. Emphasize that all people do bad things at times. That doesn't mean that they are bad people, only that they are human and made a mistake. The most important thing is to recognize and admit that you've done something wrong and learn from the experience.

Place these three signs (prepared ahead of time) on the wall:

- I think that was a very good thing to do.
- I'm not sure whether that was good or bad.
- I think that was a very bad thing to do.

Tell the students that you are going to read them some situations, and you want them to go and stand in front of the sign that matches what they think or feel about the behavior of the people in the situation. One at a time, read the items from the list below. Give the students time to decide and position themselves. Then walk up to each group and ask individual students, *Why are you standing here?*

Interview the students about their reasons for deciding the way they did. Underscore examples that demonstrate different perceptions of what happened in the situation. When values have played a clear role in someone's decision, discuss with the class how values are developed.

Have the students return to their seats. Conclude the activity with a general discussion.

Discussion Questions:

1. What's the difference between having a bad thought or feeling, and actually doing a bad thing?
2. Have you ever wished someone were dead? Suppose the person died soon after you had that thought. Would it be your fault? How do you know?
3. Have you ever felt like running away? Was it bad to feel that way? Would it be wrong to do it?
4. When you find yourself thinking about doing something bad, how do you stop yourself from doing it?
5. How do we learn the difference between good and bad, right and wrong?
6. If you know a friend is about to do something bad, should you try to stop him or her? Why or why not?
7. To what lengths should you go to stop someone from doing something wrong?
8. How about just saying, *It's not my problem,* and looking the other way?

Situations:

- Sarah, whose parents have threatened to ground her for 6 months if she doesn't get an A, cheats on the final test.
- Kevin beats up a smaller kid because the kid was bothering Kevin's sister.
- A woman whose elderly husband has been suffering for months from an incurable disease helps him commit suicide.
- A teacher makes the class stay after school and causes Lucy to miss her music lesson. On the way out the door, Lucy yells, "Thanks a lot, witch!"
- The next day, the teacher refuses to accept Lucy's homework and gives her an F for the day.
- Lucy's parents (hearing only what the teacher did) write letters to the principal and the school board, and threaten to sue the district.
- Several children taunt a man and play tricks on him because he has a disability that makes him look and talk different.
- The parents of one of the children find out about it, but don't do anything. They say it's just "innocent fun."
- The man gets fed up, traps one of the children during a prank, and holds him captive for several hours before finally letting him go.

Variations:

Consider spreading the various parts of this activity over two or three sessions with the same group. Then spend more time examining each part: good behaviors; bad behaviors; the role of values and perceptions; the differences between thinking/feeling and doing; and how ethics are developed.

Taking Control of Anger
A Counselor/Teacher Activity

Overall Purpose:

This activity helps students understand that anger is normal, and that they can learn to control their reactions to anger. In addition, the students are exposed to a range of typical responses, and are given opportunities to observe and evaluate their own behaviors in anger-provoking situations

Materials:

One copy of the experience sheet, *Chart Your Anger*, for each student

Directions:

Begin by telling the students a real story about a recent time when you got angry. For example, you might say:

I hope you don't mind if I share this with you. I was waiting in a line of cars to get on the freeway this morning and this person zoomed by me on the shoulder of the onramp. He was going so fast it looked like he was going to lose control of his car. He passed up all of us who were waiting patiently for our turn. I was furious. In fact, I still feel mad when I talk about it.

Ask the students if they ever get angry. Talk a little about the kinds of things that provoke anger in them.

Ask the students to take out a sheet of paper (or distribute paper) and write a list of events or situations that make them angry. Give the students 5 or 10 minutes to do this. When they have finished, tell them to go back through their list and number the items from "Most Angry" (#1) to "Least Angry" (highest number).

Next, return to your earlier story, and talk about your behaviors when you were angry. Continuing with the previous example, you might say:

When I was angry with that driver this morning, I started yelling. No one could hear me inside my car, but I was yelling anyway. The woman in front of me laid on her horn, and I heard a couple of other horns blaring, too.

Explain that you and the other people were expressing your anger or "blowing off steam." Point out that some ways of expressing anger are more effective than others. Also, some exhibit more self-control than others. Give the students an opportunity to talk about ways in which they express anger.

Then, have the students turn their sheet of paper over and, on the back, list things they do when they're angry. Give them another 5 to 10 minutes to complete this second list. When they have finished, tell them to go back through the list and number the items from "Most Effective" (#1) to "Least Effective" (highest number).

Ask volunteers to share their lists with the class. Discuss the effects of various expressions of anger, and the relative amounts of self-control they require.

Distribute the experience sheets. Go over the directions, and answer any questions about the use of the chart. Explain that the students are to chart their reactions to anger for 1 week. Involve the teacher in establishing the exact date on which the charts must be brought back to class.

Teacher Follow-up:

Have the students discuss their charts in small groups. Suggest that they take turns sharing one or two events from their chart, and talk about which behaviors worked for them, and which didn't. Conclude the activity with a class discussion.

Discussion Questions:

1. What similarities did you notice in the things that made us angry?
2. What were the most common reactions?
3. What are the benefits of being in control?
4. What are the dangers of reacting with low self-control?
5. What high self-control behavior would you like to learn? How can you go about learning it?

Chart Your Anger!

Student Experience Sheet

Getting angry is a reaction that comes naturally. You hardly ever have to think about it. Here's what you do have to think about: How to <u>control yourself</u> when you are angry, and how to express your anger in constructive ways. That's much harder.

Use the chart on the other side for one week. Every time you get angry, write it down. In the EVENT column, describe what happened to make you angry. In the REACTION column, put the number of the reaction that comes closest to what you did. Choose from the list below. If you did two or more things, put two or more numbers. At the end of the week, answer the questions on the other side. Then, bring your experience sheet back to class.

Reactions

LOW SELF-CONTROL

1. Physically hurt someone.
2. Damage or destroy property.
3. Use alcohol or drugs to forget about it.
4. Yell accusations or threats.
5. Call a person lots of bad names.
6. Try to get someone in trouble by telling.
7. Ignore it and pretend nothing happened.
8. Take several deep breaths.
9. Count to ten.
10. Punch a pillow or a punching bag.
11. Assertively say what you think.
12. Go for a bike ride, or play a sport or game.
13. Listen to music.
14. Take a walk, run, or swim.
15. Do a relaxation exercise or meditation.
16. Write about it in your diary or journal.
17. Share your feelings with someone you trust.

HIGH SELF-CONTROL

EVENT	REACTION

Questions:

1. Were any of the things that made you angry preventable? _____

How could they have been prevented? _____

_____

3. Which high self-control actions work best for you?

_____

4. Which high self-control actions would you like to learn?

_____

Scary Stories

A Counselor-Teacher Activity

Overall Purpose:

This activity allows you to help students express current or past anxieties and fears and explore alternative methods of coping with them. At the same time, the students have an opportunity to hone their writing and story-construction skills.

Materials:

Writing materials for the students

Directions:

If possible, have the students sit in a single large circle. Introduce the activity by acknowledging matter-of-factly that everyone is afraid sometimes. Then ask the students to think of something they're afraid of, and invite several students to tell the group what they fear. Choose one of the contributions, and suggest that the students create a group story about it. Go around the circle and have each child in turn add a sentence to the story. For example, if one of the students says, *I'm afraid of big dogs*, the story might begin something like this:

You: *I'm walking home and I see a big dog.*
First child: *The dog starts to bark at me.*
Second child: *I'm afraid the dog will bite me.*
Third child: *I cross to the other side of the street.*
Fourth child: *The dog comes after me.*
Etc.

When you have finished going around the circle, facilitate a discussion about the fear expressed and the strategies that the students came up with, as part of their story, for dealing with the fear. Ask what other strategies might have been used, and discuss alternatives. If the story becomes outlandish, point out the need for legitimate caution toward strange animals, and contrast probable and improbable events, as well as reasonable and unreasonable fears.

Next, write several story-starters on the board. For example:
"The scariest thing that ever happened to me was..."
"The most frightening place I ever visited was..."
"Once I got very afraid when..."
"Sometimes I feel scared because..."

Have the students return to their regular seats, and distribute the writing materials. Working individually, have the students select a story starter and use it to begin the first sentence of a short story. In your own words, elaborate:

Write a one-page story about your scary event. Tell who else was involved, what you did in response to your fear, and how the situation turned out.

Allow about 15 minutes for writing. Then, as time permits, invite volunteers to read their stories to the class. Use each story to stimulate discussion about fear and and various alternatives for responding to fear. Ask some of the questions below. Suggest that the teacher facilitate a follow-up sharing session for students whose stories were not heard due to lack of time.

Discussion Questions:

1. Why do people feel afraid? What good does it do?
2. What kinds of things did most of us seem to be afraid of?
3. How often do the things we fear turn out to be harmless?
4. When feelings of fear are making it hard for you to work, or play, or eat, what can you do about it?
5. When you feel afraid, whom can you talk to at home? ...at school?

Variations:

Add additional challenge and teacher involvement to the second part of the activity: Begin with a pre-writing phase in which the children share their responses to the story starters orally in small groups. Facilitate additional discussion with the total group, inviting volunteers to repeat their stories to the class. Then assign the short-story writing. In a teacher-led follow-up activity, have the students share their written stories with the class and choose one story to fictionalize. Involve the students in characterization, describing the setting and plot details, and brainstorming resolutions. Using this story and story-writing process as a model, have every student fictionalize his or her own story. Display, duplicate and distribute the stories, or bind them in a book of short stories.

On the Fear Line!

A Counselor Activity

Overall Purpose:

This activity helps students publicly acknowledge that they do have fears, understand the difference between rational and irrational fears, and consider alternative ways of handling a variety of fears.

Materials:

Paper and pencil for each child

Directions:

Announce that the subject of today's visit is "fear." Ask for a show of hands from students who have never felt afraid. If you get any hands at all, merely take note and then ask how many have felt afraid of something. Most hands will go up.

Acknowledge that it takes courage to talk about our fears, and you appreciate the willingness of students to participate.

Draw a long horizontal line on the board. At one end, draw a determined looking face and label it Fearless Fairburn. At the other end draw a frightened looking face and label it Frightened Finlay. Explain to the students that Fairburn and Finlay are at the very extreme ends of the "fear line," which means they are completely opposite each other when it comes to being afraid.

Enlist the students' help in describing Fairburn and Finlay. For example:

Fearless Fairburn eats raw meat, rides a bike down the center line with no hands, refuses to wear a seat belt, teases mean-looking dogs, and thinks it would be fun to organize a relay team to race across freeways. Frightened Finlay wears a muffler in July, trembles at the sight of a kitten, figures a cut on the finger means the end is near, and won't walk to the mailbox without a companion.

Ask the students to decide where on the line they'd place themselves compared to Fairburn and Finlay. Have volunteers come up and write their names (or draw themselves) on the line. Ask each volunteer to tell the group what led him or her to choose that spot on the line. When you run out of volunteers (or when the board gets overly crowded with names), pick the person nearest the center of the line and ask:

— *How many are more afraid than (name of student)?*
— *How many are less afraid than (name of same student)?*

Talk with the group about the difference between rational and irrational (realistic and unrealistic) fears. Point out that rational fears, such as fear of speeding cars, serve a useful purpose. They make us defensive pedestrians and bike riders. On the other hand, a fear of all cars is irrational, because it serves no useful purpose and interferes with leading a normal life.

Next, distribute the paper and ask the students to each write down two fears. Tell them not to put their names on the paper and not to tell anyone what they've written. Collect the papers.

Have the students form small groups of four or five. Shuffle the papers and divide them up among the groups. Then, in your own words, explain to the students:

Pretend that you are a committee of fear experts, and are meeting to look at some cases. Read each fear and discuss it. Decide first if you think the fear is rational or irrational, and then discuss ways of coping with or overcoming the fear. Write down your thoughts and conclusions on each slip of paper.

Allow the groups about 15 minutes to meet. Circulate and assist, as necessary. Then ask the groups to share their thoughts and conclusions with the class. Lead a culminating discussion.

Discussion Questions:

1. Were most of our fears rational or irrational?
2. How do we learn to be afraid of something?
3. What are some things that you used to be afraid of but no longer fear?
4. What did you learn that helped you outgrow your fear?
5. What new ideas did you get today for coping with a fear?

Variations:

Conduct the meeting of experts as a total group. Write the headings, "Rational" and "Irrational" (or Realistic/Unrealistic) on the board with a vertical in between. Read each fear, discuss it with the "experts" and list it under the appropriate heading.

Crises Happen!
A Counselor Activity

Overall Purpose:

This activity encourages students to utilize artistic expression to capture feelings and thoughts related to a personal crises. Through sharing and discussion, the students learn ways of better coping with crisis situations.

Materials:

Drawing paper, colored markers and/or crayons, and other art materials

Directions:

Ask the students if they know what the word crisis means. Listen to and reflect the students responses. Explain that a crisis is a time when a big change occurs in a person's life, often caused by a loss of some kind, and always accompanied by strong emotions. Give several examples of personal crises events and ask the students to think of others. Write them on the board. Your list should include:

— death of a relative
— death of a friend
— death of a pet
— parents' divorce or separation
— parent's loss of a job
— moving and leaving friends
— family illness or accident
— being hurt or abused

Distribute the art materials and ask the students to draw a picture of a personal crisis that they have experienced. Allow at least 15 minutes for this process. Then ask volunteers to share their drawing with the class, explaining details of the event and how they felt.

Facilitate discussion after each sharing. Talk in general about thoughts and feelings that people typically experience in connection with the type of crisis shared. In the process, make these points:
- Every crisis eventually passes.
- Painful, hurt feelings are gradually replaced by more positive feelings.
- Family events, such as divorce, are never the child's fault.
- There are people in the community who want to help.

Discussion Questions:

1. What kinds of thoughts did you have during your crisis?
2. Which thoughts were helpful? ...not helpful?
3. What feelings did most of us experience at times of crisis?
4. To whom can you go for help during a crisis?
5. What can you do to help yourself?
6. Why do we have a tendency to feel guilty when we lose a person or a pet we love?

Variations:

In a second phase of the activity, allow students who have experienced similar crises to meet in small groups for sharing and further discussion. Suggest that they respond to the topic, "How I Survived a Crisis."

Instead of drawing, older students may prefer to write fictionalized accounts of their crises in the form of short stories or plays. After the stories/plays have been written, ask the teacher to handle peer critiquing sessions, editing, and rewriting. Return to the class for sharing of the finished products and discussion. Students who write plays should then be given an opportunity to cast, rehearse, and present them.

Dealing with Crisis
A Counselor Activity

Overall Purpose:

Following a collective crisis — major accident, violent crime, bomb scare, riot, etc. — most if not all students benefit from group counseling activities in the classroom. The activities described below are designed to help students cope with the feelings and psychological/physical stress associated with a crisis.

Materials:

Writing paper, pencils, drawing paper, colored markers and/or crayons; colored construction paper and glue (optional)

Directions:

Distribute the writing materials. On the board write these sentence starters:

- During the _____, I felt _____.
- When I heard that _____, I felt _____.
- I still think about _____, and I feel _____.
- When I see _____, I'm reminded of _____, and I feel _____.

Have the students each choose one starter. Tell the students to complete the sentence with whatever thoughts come to mind. Allow them to add more sentences if the wish.

When most of the students have finished writing, distribute the drawing materials. In your own words, explain:

Draw a picture to illustrate the sentence(s) you've written. Depict what happened and the people involved, show yourself and your friends reacting to the event, or illustrate some other aspect that is important to you.

Have the students combine their writings and drawings (*e.g.*, by gluing both on construction-paper backing). Give the students an opportunity to share their products, either with a partner, in small groups, or with the entire class. Respect the wishes of those who decline to share. Display the finished work around the classroom.

Conclude the activity with a discussion, facilitating the expression of feelings, concerns about future events, and consideration of alternative behaviors in crisis situations.

Discussion Questions:

1. Why do you think this happened?
2. What could have been done to prevent it?
3. How can we stop something like this from happening again?
4. What have you learned from this experience?
5. What helped you most to cope with this?
6. What can you do to help others in similar situations?
7. Why is it important to talk about what happened?
8. If you continue to have strong feelings, what should you do?

Variations:

Have the students develop role plays and re-enact the crisis or components of the crisis. Use puppets to re-enact the event for very young children.

If your heart is in Social-Emotional Learning, visit us online.

Come see us at
www.InnerchoicePublishing.com

Our web site gives you a look at all our other Social-Emotional Learning-based books, free activities, articles, research, and learning and teaching strategies. Every week you'll get a new Sharing Circle topic and lesson.

INNERCHOICE Publishing
15079 Oak Chase Court
Wellington, FL 33414

www.ingramcontent.com/pod-product-compliance
Lightning Source LLC
Chambersburg PA
CBHW060315240426
43661CB00059B/2769